A COMPANION GUIDE FOR
ROSH HASHANA & YOM KIPPUR

SHANA
TOVA!

A COMPILATION OF STORIES, ESSAYS AND
DISCUSSION POINTS FOR BOTH YOUNGER AND
OLDER READERS TO BE USED ALONGSIDE A MACHZOR

Acknowledgments
We thank all authors, especially those who wrote specially for this machzor companion and the following, in particular: John Melchior of Hadley Wood Jewish community; Lady Esther Gilbert for allowing us to use materials from www.sirmartingilbert.com; Yehoshua Siskin for his translations of Sivan Rahav Meir's WhatsApp Group English language educational messages from the original Hebrew; the US professional teams for the time and effort they have put into this publication and all areas of our work; Richard Herman for his design and Kellmat Printers for printing and distribution; The Rabbinical Council of the United Synagogue (RCUS) under the stewardship of Rabbi Nicky Liss for its leadership. We also gratefully acknowledge the outstanding enterprise and dedication that our rabbis and rebbetzens have shown with so many other initiatives over the last six months, including this publication; Rabbi Andrew Shaw of Mizrachi UK for helping with materials; Finchley Synagogue (Kinloss) for providing the ideal facilities for the production of this book; Koren Publishers Jerusalem, especially Matthew Miller, Aryeh Grossman and Alex Drucker for generously partnering with us.

Image credits
P.3 – Shutterstock; P.4/5 – John Melchior; P.7/10/13/15/17/19 – Shutterstock; P.7 – Koren; P.25 – Shutterstock; P.27 – St John's Wood Synagogue; P.29 – Wikimedia; P.30/31 – Shutterstock; P.32 – Freepik; P.34 – Wikimedia; P.35 – YouTube; P.37/38/39 – Shutterstock; P.40 Koren; P.41/44/47 – Rabbi Wasserman; P.45 – Israel Government Photo Office; P.46/47/48 – Shutterstock; P.50/51/52 – Koren; P.53 – YU Archives; P.54/55 – Wikimedia; P.57/58 Lau Lavie family; P.59 – Shutterstock; P.63 – The Gilbert family; P.64 – 45 Aid Society; P.65/69 – Shutterstock; P.72 – Koren; P.73 – Wikimedia; P.74 – Raffi Berg; P.76 – Koren; P.76 – Freepik; P.79 – Shutterstock; P.80 – Centre for Israel Education; P.82 – Wikimedia; P.85 – Wikimedia; P.86 – Amia.org, The Jerusalem Institute, Wikimedia; P.87 – izkor.gov.il; P.88 – Freepik; P.89 – Paul Solomons, Freepik; P.91 – Richard Herman; P.92 – Freepik; P.93 – Freepik; P.94 – Freepik; P.95 – Paul Solomons, Freepik

KOREN
PUBLISHERS
JERUSALEM

First published in Great Britain 2020
by the United Synagogue
305 Ballards Lane, Finchley, London N12 8GB
Registered charity number 242552
info@theus.org.uk
www.theus.org.uk
©2020 United Synagogue

ISBN 978-1-909004-15-3

CONTENTS

This wonderful collection of engaging and relatable materials will help to fill the void felt by many as we adapt to an abridged synagogue service.

We hope that this book will also inspire us to bring the Shul into our family homes this Rosh Hashana and Yom Kippur.

Dedicated in the merit of our dear parents

MARLENE GREEN *z"l*

RUTH HARRIS *z"l*

DAVID HARRIS *z"l*

May this year be a Shana Tova U'metuka for us all.

In loving memory of

IRVING CARTER *z"l*

A man that put his family, his community and his commitment to charity at the heart of everything he did.

The trustees of the

ROSEMARIE NATHANSON CHARITABLE TRUST

are honoured to support this book and wish you all Shana Tova

FOREWORD

Many people are not aware that Yom Kippur is actually an anniversary. It takes place every year on the day when, according to our tradition, Moshe came down from Mount Sinai for the second time.

As is widely known, on the first occasion, he descended from the mountain to witness the Children of Israel worshipping the golden calf and he smashed the sacred tablets. Moshe ascended Mount Sinai again on the first day of the month of Elul. After forty more days and nights, he descended on the tenth of Tishrei. That day became the original Yom Hakippurim, a day of atonement for our people.

Like Yom Kippur, all of the other celebrations and commemorations on our calendar take place on anniversaries, with just one exception - the festival of Succot.

The Torah gives God's reason for Succot as follows: "Because I caused the Israelites to dwell in booths when I brought them out of the land of Egypt" (Vayikra 23:42).

So, the ideal time for Succot would, in fact, be when we celebrate Pesach! Our tradition saves us from the challenge of staging a Seder in a succah, but, if Succot was to be moved to another time of the year, surely it should be in a quiet month when nothing much else is happening?

After we conclude a whole month of careful introspection during Elul, followed immediately by Rosh Hashana, the Ten Days of Penitence and Yom Kippur, we celebrate Succot just five days later. From the first day of the month of Elul until Simchat Torah, there is no let-up - could God not have given us a bit of a break?

Anyone with experience of planning special events or impactful educational programmes will appreciate the reason for this. The most crucial aspect of an important event or happening must be the follow-up. A one-off experience can be profoundly exhilarating, but if nothing follows it, what has it really achieved? Similarly, our spiritual development is not an event; it is a process.

Over the Yamim Noraim we undertake a 'Cheshbon Hanefesh' - an 'accounting of the soul'. We take time to examine the current trajectory of our lives. Do we feel that we are on the right path? Do we need to correct our course? God then provides us with an immediate opportunity to translate our aspirations into reality; to turn our resolutions into meaningful action. He gives us the gift of Succot.

We enter 5781 in the most extraordinary circumstances. Many are starting to return to Shul for the first time since the Covid-19 pandemic hit. Others will continue to remain at home to protect themselves and others. For all of us, this period presents us with an opportunity to begin to get back to the spiritual work that we may have been kept from in recent months.

Wherever you are for Rosh Hashana and Yom Kippur, please ensure that neither is merely an event that comes and goes, but the start of a meaningful, uplifting and fulfilling process which never ends.

I wish you all ketiva vechatimah tovah,   כתיבה וחתימה טובה

Chief Rabbi Ephraim Mirvis
Elul 5780/August 2020

WELCOME TO SHANA TOVA!

What is this book?

Shana Tova!, a companion guide for the Yamim Noraim, or Shana Tova! for short, is a new publication from the United Synagogue, following on from Shabbat Shalom! published last year. In my role as President and on behalf of all the US Trustees, with thanks to God, I am delighted to introduce this publication to you. We thank all of our sponsors for their generosity and kindness. May God bless them in all that they do.

Shana Tova! is a wide-ranging compilation of stories, essays and discussion points for both younger and older readers to be used alongside a machzor (Yom Tov prayer book) whether you are in shul, at home or around your Yom Tov table. Some of it is specially written, whilst a number of pieces have been compiled from pre-existing publications. Due to the inclusion of sacred Hebrew texts, please treat this book with the sanctity required for a prayer book. The Hebrew texts are brief excerpts from our prayers, provided as references to help readers link to the prayers in the machzor.

The machzor is a guide through the prayers and themes of the day. In particular, Shana Tova! complements the outstanding Koren Sacks "Minhag Anglia" machzorim with an introduction, translation and explanatory notes by Rabbi Lord Jonathan Sacks. They both have the same dimensions and we hope that Shana Tova! will find a place on your bookshelf for future years alongside your machzor.

Please also visit the Yamim Noraim pages on our website at www.theus.org.uk/shanatova and our TV site www.theus.tv for further information, materials and programmes about Rosh Hashana and Yom Kippur.

The Jewish year ending at the time of writing, 5780 (2019-2020), has not been an easy one for us, our communities or the world. Sadly, too many Jews will not be able to observe and celebrate the Yamim Noraim in a community setting.

As we look forward to a new year, we ask God to bless us and the whole world, to answer our prayers for the good and hope that the provisions provided by your local shul and the US centrally help you to feel more connected than otherwise.

I wish you and yours well. Shana tova!

May God provide us all with a good and sweet year, written and sealed in the book of life   יהי רצון שתתחדש עלינו שנה טובה ומתוקה כתיבה וחתימה טובה

Michael Goldstein
President of the United Synagogue
Elul 5780/August 2020

DAYS OF AWE   ימים נוראים

Together, Rosh Hashana and Yom Kippur are known as the Yamim Noraim (Days of Awe) due to the sanctity and particular awareness of the presence of God which we feel during these days. They are also great days of community, both inside and outside the synagogue, when many Jews 'return home' even if they have not connected to a community during the previous year.

ROSH HASHANA

- A Yom Tov, the start of the year, occurring on 1 & 2 Tishrei in the Jewish calendar

- Famous for the mitzva (commandment) to blow the Shofar, special prayers and tunes to express the holiness of this time.

- A time of judgement and self-improvement, whilst reaffirming our acceptance of God.

- Well-known culinary customs such as eating apple with honey to signify our wish for a sweet new year.

- Start of the window of opportunity called the Aseret Yemei Teshuva, 10 days of repentance, culminating on Yom Kippur. During this time, we seek extra opportunities to perform mitzvot, such as increased, impactful prayer, charitable activities and acts of kindness.

- A good time to set aspirations for the year ahead and how we are going to make the world a better place in the year ahead, through the Judaism we practise.

YOM KIPPUR

- The holiest day of the year, a fast day, occurring on 10 Tishrei in the Jewish calendar.

- A day of forgiveness, prayer and contemplation on which God grants us a fresh start.

- It is up to us to make the most of this. To help us focus on the meaning and opportunity afforded by Yom Kippur, we become like angels through fasting and abstaining from various physical pleasures or adornments such as not wearing leather shoes. There is also a widespread custom to wear at least one white item of clothing.

- A time when we remember those who came before us, through reciting the Yizkor prayers.

- Five prayer services, starting with Kol Nidre as Yom Kippur enters and ending with Neila as Yom Kippur draws to a close.

- A day of hope and joy, despite the fast, due to the forgiveness and opportunities to start again which we request for the year ahead.

CANDLE LIGHTING

(i) Before the start of Shabbat and Yom Tov, including Rosh Hashana and Yom Kippur, we light candles in honour of these days. The blessings for Rosh Hashana are below.

On both nights, say the following blessing and then light the candles.
On the second night, the candles must be lit from an existing flame.
If the first day of ראש השנה is שבת, cover the eyes with the hands after lighting
the candles and say the following blessing, adding the words in parentheses.

בָּרוּךְ Blessed are You, LORD our God, King of the Universe,
who has made us holy through His commandments,
and has commanded us to light
(the Sabbath light and) the festival light.

בָּרוּךְ אַתָּה יהוה אֱלֹהֵינוּ מֶלֶךְ הָעוֹלָם
אֲשֶׁר קִדְּשָׁנוּ בְּמִצְוֹתָיו
וְצִוָּנוּ לְהַדְלִיק נֵר שֶׁל (שַׁבָּת וְשֶׁל) יוֹם טוֹב.

The blessing "Sheheḥeyanu" ("Who has given us life") is said on both evenings.

The blessing שֶׁהֶחֱיָנוּ is said on both evenings.

בָּרוּךְ Blessed are You, LORD our God, King of the Universe,
who has given us life, sustained us, and brought us to this time.

בָּרוּךְ אַתָּה יהוה אֱלֹהֵינוּ מֶלֶךְ הָעוֹלָם
שֶׁהֶחֱיָנוּ וְקִיְּמָנוּ, וְהִגִּיעָנוּ לַזְּמַן הַזֶּה.

What do you think of when lighting these candles? Why? Why do we light candles at the start of our special days?

The Longest-Running Torah Class

As told to Sivan Rahav Meir

halom, my name is Reuven Ben-Porat and I feel compelled to share the story of my grandmother, Esther. 63 years ago, in 1956, Grandma Esther was asked to conduct a Torah class on Shabbat for women who were living in a transit camp for new immigrants near Haifa. The class was originally taught in French for the benefit of immigrants from North Africa, but later was taught in Hebrew for immigrants who came from Yemen, Persia, France, the Soviet Union, Ethiopia, and from other countries, too. Esther walked to the class every Shabbat, without ever taking a break. During the Gulf War, for example, the class was not interrupted, but conducted in a bomb shelter.

This year, Grandma Esther celebrated her 100th birthday and, lately, has

declined in health and become weaker. This Shabbat, for the first time, she will not be conducting the class. This is what she wrote to class attendees, both past and present.

"God gave me two great gifts of love: love for the Torah and love for the Jewish people. These two wonderful gifts I have tried to utilise for the benefit of us all. We learned Torah together, but we also learned about our many different customs and traditions, out of deep respect for each person in attendance. With sad regret, because of my health, I am forced at the present time to retire from my role as the teacher of the class. Thank you for all the 'together' moments created during more than 60 years. May we merit to see the coming redemption very soon."

This is my grandmother and I do not believe there is another Torah class in the whole world that has endured so many years, conducted by the same teacher. In an age when governments rise and fall in quick succession, and the subjects of arguments and protests continuously change, I want people to know about Grandma Esther and her class. And, appropriately, all of us, like Esther, light little flames, one day after the next, with persistence, a demonstration of our connection to eternal values.

A Miracle

As we light our candles for Rosh Hashana, it is timely to cast our thoughts back to an Erev Rosh Hashana where the Jews in Denmark faced the worst fear you could imagine. This is the story of how the population in one country saved their Jewish population, as told by **Rabbi Bent Melchior.**

Rabbi Melchior

In the autumn of 1943, I was a boy of fourteen. Until then, the Jews of Denmark had lived under occupation in the same conditions as the rest of the population, but as soon as the Danish government resigned, the Germans began to persecute the Jewish population. We were lucky that one of the Germans, a man called Georg Duckwitz, communicated to some Danish politicians that the Jews would be deported, three days ahead of the operation. They in turn warned the Jewish community. That was a Tuesday, a few days before Rosh Hashana.

I was the son of a rabbi and since the Chief Rabbi had been arrested, the message from Duckwitz was delivered to my father. I remember that Tuesday night, just before curfew, a secretary to one of the Danish politicians arrived at our home and gave us the bad news. It was not possible to do anything that evening during curfew. We could not use the phone, as we feared that all our calls were being listened to by the Germans.

The next morning, many members of the community were present for the Selichot service in the synagogue. My father stopped the service at a certain point and said, "We have no time now to continue prayers. We know that this coming Friday night, Erev Rosh Hashana, the Gestapo will come and arrest all Danish Jews. They will come to the home of every Jew and take us all to two big ships waiting in Copenhagen harbour, and on to camps on the continent."

He told everyone, "There are two things you should do. Firstly, you should stay away from your homes on Friday night. Secondly, pass this news onto as many friends, family, whomever you can, so that they also know to leave home by Friday."

That got the ball rolling. We tried in so many ways to contact people. We could not explain on the telephone what was going on, but I remember my mother phoning friends saying that we had decided to go to the country for a few days for a vacation, and we needed the fresh air. And because everybody knew that a rabbi

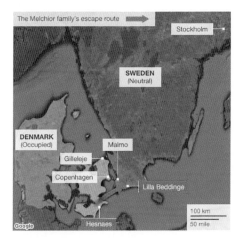

The Melchior route to freedom

would not leave town for Rosh Hashana, they understood the message. It was decided to close the synagogue for the New Year. That was another way of telling people something was going on.

I had 4 siblings, 3 older and 1 younger. We all heard my parents discuss what to do. After spreading the news, the question became: where should we go? We knew that ultimately we had to get to Sweden which was neutral and not occupied. At the narrowest point, there were only a few miles of sea between Denmark and Sweden.

My parents' first thought was not about escaping Denmark but where we could hide. It is not so easy when there are six of you. (My oldest brother had already fled to Sweden.) You could not knock on your neighbours' doors and ask if they had room. Eventually my parents decided to go to a small village ninety kilometres away where my father knew the priest. We did not dare phone him, so we just went and hoped he could find us a place to hide.

Danish fishing boat in the 1940s

We went to the train station. We could not carry much with us, because that would of course raise suspicion. I remember, I had my own little bag that I took to school every day, in which I put some clothes and a maths book. It was a very emotional moment when we closed the door to our apartment, not knowing whether we ever would see it again or what would become of us. That moment influenced me for the rest of my life.

We arrived at the priest's village and telephoned him. He immediately understood what was going on and said, "Come! Come!" He had no thoughts of trying to contact any members of his community. We would all stay at his place, he had plenty of room. He said we could stay there until the end of the war. He was a marvellous man, I recall. A strong man, who knew what he was dealing with and knew how dangerous it was to help Jews trying to escape from the Gestapo.

That night the German raid was carried out. Out of around eight thousand Jews in Denmark, the Germans found only about two hundred people in their homes. Some of them had heard the news but refused to believe it. Some, we were not able to reach. But it was a pretty good result, getting over 97% informed and away in 2 days. 7800 Jews were now dispersed among private homes, or in hospitals, or wherever they could find a place to hide. Nobody was prepared for this, nothing had been organised in advance, so this was truly a grassroots movement of people taking matters into their own hands, who saw to it that we were kept away from the Germans.

In a small town everybody would have known he was hiding us, but nobody there would dream of giving us up to the Germans.

The next step of the operation was to build an organisation and to find boats that could take us over to Sweden. A very high percentage succeeded. Sadly, a few drowned on the way and a number were captured by German guards. About eighty Jews were captured in a local church near Elsinore after someone gave away information about their hiding place. Altogether around five hundred Danish Jews were taken to the Theresienstadt Concentration Camp and around fifty did not return. Even in the camps, the Danish government insisted on sending food packages through the Red Cross movement and monitored the wellbeing of their countrymen.

Although food was rationed and you could not buy all the meat or sugar that you wanted, we had saved up some meat for the holidays, which we took with us. In the country, you could get the basics, bread and vegetables and the priest had a wonderful apple orchard.

Although you could trust the people in the village and there were very few German soldiers around, it could not be kept secret forever now that

the priest was suddenly buying for six more people to eat. The question was whether to stay or move on, and when. And after the capture of the 80 people in the church, the Resistance movement advised that we would have to go to the southern part of Denmark where the journey to Sweden would be much longer. It was not a question of comfort or convenience, but of survival. On 8 October, we left our priest and travelled south where we were to meet the local bishop, who immediately recognised my father and embraced him. This was the day before Yom Kippur and I remember the bishop asked my father, "Is there anything special Jews eat on this day?" He wanted us to have the chance to observe our rules as much as possible, despite the circumstances. He had at that time sixty Jews hidden at his place, so there was already great danger. In a small town everybody would have known he was hiding us, but nobody there would dream of giving us up to the Germans.

The fishermen in the village who were helping Jews to get to Sweden were fearful. Their boats were their livelihood. If the Germans caught them, their boats would be confiscated and they would have no way to feed their families. So they asked for payment as a kind of insurance policy. What they asked for was more money than we had. My elder brother went back to Copenhagen together with the bishop's son and together they managed to raise the necessary money. It was the gift of someone who would not accept repayment and given on condition that no one ever mention it. That was a marvellous gesture.

The next evening, the people of this little town guided all the Jews hiding at the bishop's house to three different places along the coast of this southern island of Denmark. Nineteen of us were in one spot, where a boat was waiting. We boarded the boat, and hid in the hold, normally used for herrings which was not very pleasant. The trip should take between six and eight hours. After almost eight hours, at three in the morning, we saw land, but the fisherman did not want to land until it was light, and the Swedes could pick us up.

I remember I was praying. With the boat lying still we were getting seasick and it seemed that God did not hear my prayers. Eventually we saw the sun and realised that it was not rising where we thought it would be. It turned out that the fisherman really did not know how to navigate at night and had gone in a circle and the land we saw was Denmark. So, once again we set off following the sun towards Sweden.

Although I was young, this was no adventure in the enjoyable sense. To be a refugee, even in a country where you have been welcomed, is a terrible thing.

Low on fuel, the miracle finally happened, and we reached Sweden on Yom Kippur 1943. Luckily a little boy was playing on the beach and managed to alert some adults to come and pick us up. It was nearly as exciting for them as it was for us and that little boy who still lives in the same house has become a lifelong and close friend.

Then the bureaucracy of being a refugee began but we knew that Sweden had said that they would accept all Danish Jews. The worry was more where could we live, how could we find work and what our new lives as refugees would be like? We ended up in Southern Sweden and I was able to continue my education in a newly formed Danish school.

The Danish Jews in Sweden together with the resistance fighters formed a Danish Brigade who prepared to take up battle with the Germans at the end of the war. Luckily the Germans gave up thanks to British Field Marshal Montgomery on 5 May 1945. The Danish Brigade immediately returned to Denmark and performed the role of policemen for some time as the Danish police had been abolished by the Germans

A few weeks later we all returned and were received as heroes – which we were not. But the Danes really appreciated our coming back. My father used to say that, as Jews, we had often experienced people being happy to see the back of us. But here was a case where the population was happy to see us returning. Our landlord kept all his promises to us, had let out our flat and protected all our furniture and belongings. Within three months we could move back in and that was, of course, an extraordinary, happy moment. Most Jews found their homes and belongings untouched when they returned.

Although I was young, this was no adventure in the enjoyable sense. To be a refugee, even in a country where you have been welcomed, is a terrible thing. You are nobody. Even when your hosts are good, there is a certain envy, "These refugees come and they take our good things." In my adult life, I have worked for the cause of refugees in Denmark to the extent that I have become the first and only honorary member of the Danish Refugee Council. That was the outcome of what I experienced being a refugee myself in Sweden.

In Denmark, we, the Jews were always regarded as normal citizens. If a neighbour was being persecuted, you helped your neighbour. You did not help because of an order from some authority or because somebody told you. Although the church decreed that it was a duty to help the Jews, the Danes did it because we were fellow Danes and fellow human beings in need of help.

And that is still so. In February 2015, we experienced the tragedy of a Jewish guard being shot by a terrorist outside the synagogue in Copenhagen. During the following period, thousands of ordinary people walked past the synagogue, leaving notes and flowers, stopping to pay their respect. I saw that these were the same people that rescued us so many years ago and once again I realised how lucky and proud I was to be a Danish Jew.

KIDDUSH FOR ROSH HASHANA EVENING AND SIMANIM

קִידוּשׁ לְלֵיל רֹאשׁ הַשָּׁנָה וְסִימָנִים

ⓘ Kiddush, recited before Shabbat and Yom Tov dinner, acts as an introduction to and sanctification of these holy days. On Rosh Hashana, our practice is to eat various symbolic foods (simanim) at the start of the meal, such as pomegranates, honey (with the challah) and carrots as a way of giving another form of expression to our prayers, hopes and aspirations for the year ahead.

On the first night, following Kiddush and "HaMotzi," an apple is dipped in honey and the following is said:

בָּרוּךְ Blessed are You, LORD our God, King of the Universe, who creates the fruit of the tree.

After eating some of the apple and honey, say:

יְהִי רָצוֹן May it be Your will, LORD our God and God of our ancestors, that You renew for us a good and sweet year.

On the first night, following קִידוּשׁ and הַמּוֹצִיא,
an apple is dipped in honey and the following is said:

בָּרוּךְ אַתָּה יהוה אֱלֹהֵינוּ מֶלֶךְ הָעוֹלָם, בּוֹרֵא פְּרִי הָעֵץ.

After eating some of the apple and honey, say:

יְהִי רָצוֹן מִלְּפָנֶיךָ יהוה אֱלֹהֵינוּ וֵאלֹהֵי אֲבוֹתֵינוּ
שֶׁתְּחַדֵּשׁ עָלֵינוּ שָׁנָה טוֹבָה וּמְתוּקָה.

Why is food important in teaching and practising Judaism? What are your favourite Jewish foods and why? What does your family eat specially for Rosh Hashana and why?

Sign of the Times

Rebbetzen Ilana Epstein

Special times have special signs. Rosh Hashana is no different. As we usher in a new year, we bring resonant messages of Rosh Hashana to our Yom Tov table, blending the physical and spiritual as we set out our hopes for the year ahead.

We do this through the colourful traditions of the simanim (signs or 'omens'), foods that we eat on Rosh Hashana. Each food is accompanied by a special prayer, stating our aspirations for a prosperous and good year ahead.

In many families, especially those of Sephardic origin, this is a much honoured and loved tradition which, until recently, was mostly commonly associated with Sephardic homes. Yet it played a big part in the Ashkenazi home I grew up in and is a tradition that my Jerusalem-born Ashkenazi grandfather was very proud to call his own, as long as my Sephardic grandmother made every dish in her 'special' way. Today, many homes have adopted the customs and various versions of the simanim. The associated blessings can be found in many machzorim just after Kiddush on the first night of Rosh Hashana.

... We bring resonant messages of Rosh Hashana to our Yom Tov table, blending the physical and spiritual as we set out our hopes for the year ahead.

We first learn of the simanim from the Talmud, (Keritut 6b), the great work of Jewish law and ethics which, when discussing simanim, notes that 'a person should always be accustomed on Rosh Hashana to see or eat gourd, fenugreek, leek, beets and dates'. These were not the 'staple' foods for many people and would stand out on Rosh Hashana. The scholar Rashi (d.1105), in explaining the reason for these foods, noted that they either grow rapidly or taste sweet; thus they are simanim for a year of abundance of mazal and of sweetness.

The names of the food items themselves are significant. A number of them – such as my favourite, "rubia" (fenugreek) – are a play on words for the Hebrew word "leharbot", meaning abundance or increase. We thereby ask God that our merits and good deeds should increase. The foods used for the simanim have developed over the centuries. The renowned 17th century Rabbi Avraham Gombiner used rubia to set a precedent, stating that any food which sounds like the word for abundance in any language may be used.

One historical custom associated with Rosh Hashana is the ancient practice of eating meats and drinking sweet beverages as simanim for a prosperous and sweet new year. The Geonim, the leading scholars of Babylonia between approximately 500-1000CE, trace this custom back to the time of the Second Temple in Jerusalem. The scholar Ezra stood before the people on the first day of the seventh month (Rosh Hashana) and read to them from the Torah. The people were distraught to realise that they were not upholding God's laws. Ezra told them not to be sad and he went on to implore them to 'go, eat rich foods [i.e. meat] and drink sweet beverages... for today is sacred to the Lord' (Nechemia 8:10). Ezra helped the people reclaim Rosh Hashana. We recall this by eating these foods, pushing us to reflect on our need to reconnect to Jewish practice in the year ahead.

Even the simple act of dipping a piece of challah in honey reminds me each year, that once I have prayed and asked God for a good year ahead...

What is the origin of perhaps the most popular of the simanim, apple dipped in honey?

The source for this is also post-Talmudic. During the Middle Ages, the Tur, a medieval work which is an early compilation of Jewish laws, records an old Ashkenazi custom to eat 'at the beginning of the meal, some sweet apple dipped in honey, over which we would say 'we should be renewed with a sweet year'. It is striking how tenaciously Jewish communities have held onto this practice for hundreds of years.

What I, as a food connoisseur, find particularly interesting is the Tur's description of how the Jews of Provence came up with new simanim for Rosh Hashana including grapes, red apples, figs and a calf's head.

Many of us will eat carrots, especially carrots cut to look like coins. One of the reasons for this is that the Yiddish word for carrots is mehren, which is similar to the Yiddish word "mehr", meaning "more". In a similar vein, even though it elicits a groan from the table every year, my husband will put out a dish with raisins and celery before looking up wistfully and saying – "May we be blessed this year with a "raisin celery", i.e. a raise in salary!

My favourite custom by far on Rosh Hashana is perhaps the simplest. The rabbinic works Levush and Kaf HaChayim mention another old, familiar Ashkenazi custom, of dipping challah in honey rather than salt. This custom is another way of mixing physical and spiritual, associating the mitzva of eating bread with our prayers for a sweet year (given that the challah also contains salt, we also adhere to eating salt with bread, to remind us of the

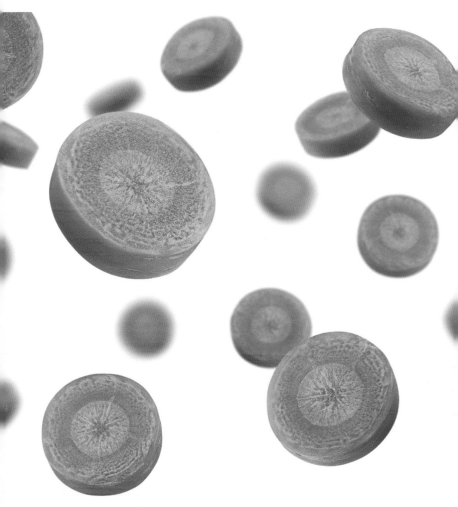

practices in the Temple). This particular custom has proved so popular that it continues throughout the festivals at this time, from the first night Rosh Hashana until Hoshana Rabba (the day before Shemini Atzeret) or, in some communities, until the last meal on Simchat Torah.

The High Holy Days are filled with prayer and ritual. Yet, that is not all that they contain. Even the simple act of dipping a piece of challah in honey reminds me each year that once I have prayed and asked God for a good year ahead, it is in my power to be a partner with God in my life and strive to enjoy blessings and abundance in the year to come.

I wish you all a sweet year ahead, blessed in every good way!

Articulating the Importance of our Closest Relationships

Rabbi Jason Kleiman

Birthdays, and anniversaries in particular, are a good time for reflection. They provide an annual focus for those celebrating, as well as for their family and friends to take stock of the importance of relationships and how these have developed. Hopefully, such occasions prompt people to express in words their love and appreciation for each other, to articulate the special nature of such relationships through the spoken word or the sentiments we convey in greeting cards.

Rosh Hashana is both a birthday celebration and a wedding anniversary. It marks the birthday of the creation of human beings and the beginning of our relationship with God, which Jewish teachings sometimes portray through the metaphor of marriage. This is why the Jewish people greet the Divine presence on Friday night in terms of welcoming the Shabbat bride and Jewish men adorned with the tefillin relate to God as a marriage partner when reciting the words: "I will betroth you to me forever."

Both our relationships with God and with each other require a specific annual appraisal during the "Days of Awe" period, as the time of Rosh Hashana and Yom Kippur is known. At this time, we ought to ask ourselves the following question: "Have we expressed our love to those who are most important in our world?".

Rosh Hashana is the perfect opportunity to tell those who are most important to us of our love for them…

It was Shakespeare who said, "They do not love that do not show their love."

Rosh Hashana is the perfect opportunity to tell those who are most important to us of our love for them and to do it not only at the start, but also throughout every day of the coming year. A constant appreciation of our cherished relationships is part of the lesson derived from the literal translation of Rosh Hashana, "Head of the Year." If we compare the course of a year to the human body, the brain is the source of all the messages that are carried to all the other organs and limbs. Similarly, the "head" of 5781 should inform all of our thoughts and actions throughout every day of the rest of the year.

Maintaining our recognition of our close relationships requires sensitivity and a readiness to have an open heart towards those around us, including God. Our task for 5781 can be learned from King Solomon, who upon becoming King, dreamed that God asked him what he most desired. King Solomon's primary request, "Please God, grant me a listening heart" (1 Kings 3:9), was granted with favour by God.

For each of us to make the coming year what it should be, we need God's help to acquire a listening heart of understanding and love that will be a source of blessing and joy to those who love us most. I wish you shana tova, a good year ahead.

From Jerusalem to Scotland: A New Year with New Beginnings

Rabbi Aharon & Hodaya Lemberger

In August 2019, we arrived in Glasgow from Israel with our three children as the University Jewish Chaplaincy couple for Scotland, just weeks before Rosh Hashana. A new country, new community, a new adventure far away from home, to begin a long-awaited opportunity to help a Jewish community overseas.

Launching into our preparations for Rosh Hashana and Yom Kippur, which included making sure all the students were welcome in our house and especially working out how to cook for so many people, we were filled with both excitement and anxiety. This was our first opportunity to celebrate a very different kind of Rosh Hashana and Yom Kippur, far away from home like many of the students.

We were delighted to see many students come to pray on the first night of Rosh Hashana at the warm and welcoming Giffnock & Newlands Synagogue in Glasgow, before coming to our house for dinner.

This was our first opportunity to celebrate a very different kind of Rosh Hashana and Yom Kippur, far away from home like many of the students.

For Yom Kippur, we travelled to Edinburgh to connect with students there. It was incredible to host over 50 students for the pre-fast meal. The students also received a warm welcome at the Edinburgh Hebrew Congregation, where Neila prayers were particularly memorable.

We were also determined to provide accessible programming for the wider cross-section of Jewish students in Edinburgh, not just those who would come to the synagogue, and facilitated an inclusive explanatory session on campus during the fast.

This was the first time that we did not spend the majority of Yom Kippur praying in shul. We will remember it and our first year on campus in the UK, especially since our work gave us opportunities to help and connect with other Jews in ways that were mutually inspiring.

TORAH READINGS

קְרִיאַת הַתּוֹרָה

ⓘ The main Torah readings for Rosh Hashana (Bereishit ch.21-22) focus on the birth and development of Yitzchak (Isaac) and the Akeda (Binding of Isaac), the last of Abraham's tests. The maftir lists the offerings given in the Temple on Rosh Hashana. The haftarah for the first day is the story of Chana (Hannah) and the birth of Shmuel (Samuel). On the second day, we read of Rachel's tears and the promises of redemption made by Yirmiyahu (Jeremiah) after the destruction of the First Temple.

 What does this challenging episode tell us about commitment to an ideal? What does it say to you about God's role in our lives? Why do you think we read it on Rosh Hashana,? What does it have to do with Rosh Hashana?

Concentric Circles

Rebbetzen Lauren Levin

Various suggestions are offered in the Talmud (Megilla 31a) as to which Torah passage we should read on the first day of Rosh Hashana. We follow the custom of reading about Yitzchak's birth, although no reason is given for this in the Talmud. Rashi (1040-1105) explains that the topic is chosen because God 'remembered' Sarah, Rachel and Chana on Rosh Hashana and they all conceived at this time (see Talmud Rosh Hashana 11a). It is logical to read the story of the birth of Sarah's child for the Torah reading and match it with that of Chana in the haftarah.

However, this only explains the beginning of the reading. After the birth of Yitzchak, we continue to read of his older, wilder brother Yishmael's fate and Avraham's treaty with the neighbouring leader Avimelech. Why are these additional two stories relevant?

Reading about Yishmael being banished and his near death raises a difficult question. Perhaps the Yishmael story comes as an epilogue to Yitzchak's birth. The miraculous nature of Yitzchak's conception and birth seems to be a happy ending to the Avraham and Sarah story. However, there was significant 'fall-out' from this. By moving straight on from the euphoria to the more thorny issues at home with Yishmael, we are made cognisant that Sarah and Yitzchak were not in a vacuum. Their new destiny had to fit back into the bigger family picture.

The next story is about the treaty made between Avraham and Avimelech.

We all have our dreams, ambitions, fears and challenges. These are the key to forming our vision for the coming year...

When Avraham first encountered Avimelech he did not reveal that Sarah was actually his wife, out of fear that Avimelech would kill him and abduct her (Bereishit 20:1-16). Avraham tried to remain insular and keep himself to himself. Yet Sarah was nevertheless taken away. Perhaps Avraham reflected that looking inwards was not the best approach. The way he conducted himself in this new encounter with Avimelech shows a dramatic change. Avraham proactively approached Avimelech and the section ends by describing Avraham "calling out to God" in the Land. Avraham can now share his love of God with the world.

As such, these three stories form concentric circles. The protagonists (Sarah and Yitzchak) and their dreams are in the middle, with Yishmael representing other family members around them, and Avimelech representing the wider society around that.

The Talmudic Sages' choice of this narrative for Rosh Hashana focuses our perspective as we enter the New Year. The intense introspection of the High Holydays is unique to every individual. We all have our dreams, ambitions, fears and challenges. These are the key to forming our vision for the coming year, but they alone are insufficient. The Yishmael narrative reminds us to align our own individual introspection alongside the broader framework of our family, friends and community. The Avimelech narrative reminds us that our visual field must go still beyond this, aiming to share and synchronise our talents and passions with the world at large.

The Real War

Sivan Rahav Meir

What is the most difficult war? The war to develop and perfect our personality. So claimed Rabbi Yisrael Salanter, who passed away 137 years ago. He established an educational movement in the Jewish world, the Mussar (moral conduct) movement, whose purpose is to change and improve a person's character traits. Here are just a few short, piercing thoughts from the many that make up Rabbi Salanter's powerful legacy.

"It is easier to master the entire Talmud than to change a single character trait."

"The material distress and physical needs of another are the spiritual concerns of mine."

"Whoever wishes to rise above someone else should not dig his friend a pit but rather construct a mountain for himself."

"Not everything we think should we say, not everything we say should we write, and not everything we write should we publish."

"It is part of human nature that the more we benefit someone else, the more we love that person with our whole heart."

AVINU MALKEINU

ℹ️ Recited on fast days and during the Aseret Yemei Teshuva (the days from Rosh Hashana and Yom Kippur, inclusive), this emotional prayer, relating to God as both our Father and our King, dates back to Rabbi Akiva in the 2nd century CE.

אָבִינוּ מַלְכֵּנוּ Our Father, our King, we have sinned before You.

Our Father, our King, we have no king but You.

Our Father, our King, deal kindly with us for the sake of Your name.

אָבִינוּ מַלְכֵּנוּ, חָטָאנוּ לְפָנֶיךָ.

אָבִינוּ מַלְכֵּנוּ, אֵין לָנוּ מֶלֶךְ אֶלָּא אָתָּה.

אָבִינוּ מַלְכֵּנוּ, עֲשֵׂה עִמָּנוּ לְמַעַן שְׁמֶךָ.

How do you understand the phrase 'Avinu Malkeinu', our Father our King, and why do we refer to God in this way? What does this tell us about being Jewish? How do you think Rabbi Amital, in the article on page 22, would answer these questions?

Avinu Malkeinu

Rabbi Dr Harvey Belovski

As the new Jewish year arrives, the motif of divine sovereignty emerges in our prayers. References to God as 'Melech' (King) pop up throughout our festival liturgy and the shofar blasts announce God's coronation.

Yet our interest in sovereignty is often confined to a pageantry and the royal family. We might think of Crown Jewels, robes and palaces – the trappings of a celebrity constitutional monarchy. We have little experience of and some discomfort around the notion of an absolute ruler. Perhaps this is why sovereignty is often combined with parenthood, as in the description of God as 'Avinu Malkeinu' (our Father, our King). God does not tyrannise humanity, but tempers what He demands of us with love and kindness. This allows us to preserve a degree of autonomy and flexibility while realising the personal and communal aspirations that the Torah sets for us. I believe that this construct is unique to Judaism and should be a cause for celebration each year.

Rabbi K.K. Shapira, famous for his profound and inspirational teachings in the Warsaw Ghetto during World War Two before his tragic murder in the Holocaust, suggests that by Succot, two weeks into the year, the emphasis shifts towards self-mastery, one of the ultimate objectives of religious life.

How so? We need first to experience heightened self-awareness in the light of the overwhelming presence of God on Rosh Hashana and Yom Kippur before we can direct our individual and collective capabilities to a more customised experience within a traditional Jewish framework of our laws and beliefs.

Each new year, we are offered an opportunity by the shofar and our prayers – especially Avinu Malkeinu – to experience a moment of transformation

The beauty of self-mastery is that it is independent of place and circumstance – ultimately, it is something we can develop whoever we are and wherever we may be: with our families, far away from home, on campus, or even alone. Yet each new year, we are offered an opportunity by the shofar and our prayers – especially Avinu Malkeinu - to experience a moment of transformation, in which we renew our relationship with God, Judaism and ourselves.

Avinu Malkeinu

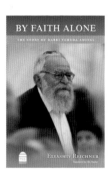

Elyashiv Reichner

Rabbi Yehuda Amital (1924-2010, originally Klein),
founder of the Har Etzion Yeshiva in Alon Shvut, Israel,
was born in Romania. Having survived the Holocaust, he
yearned to reach the Land of Israel, which he reached at
the end of 1944. In this abridged extract from 'By Faith
Alone, the story of Rabbi Yehuda Amital', we learn of Rabbi Amital's experiences in
1944 as the Hungarian guards of the forced labour camp where he was imprisoned,
tried to escape approaching Soviet forces.

Two days before Yom Kippur, as they were in the midst of reciting Selichot for the Ten Days of Repentance, the group received an order to return to camp at Grosswardein, where the Hungarian army was preparing for the invasion of the Soviets. The group marched all night in heavy rain, drawing strength from the Torah scroll that they carried. All night, they passed the scroll amongst themselves. When Yehuda's turn came to carry the Torah, he felt that it was pouring strength into him and encouraging him as he walked toward the unknown.

The group reached Grosswardein on the day before Yom Kippur. One of the two commanders left them at the train station as he went to clarify who they should join up with. The group members decided to take the opportunity to flee. Yehuda, as usual, did not believe in fleeing, but since all the members of the group had scattered, he fled as well and hid with several other boys in the vineyards, not far from the city. Most members of the group were discovered quite quickly by the gentile residents of the city and held for the irate commander, who threatened them with death. The prisoners tried to bribe their commander to release them and exempt them from punishment, but he refused and led them toward the battalion headquarters. At that exact moment, the report of combat weapons was heard. The commanders, who realised that the Soviets had arrived, abandoned the prisoners and fled in confusion.

Yehuda and his friends were left alone, without commanders. For the first time in several months, they felt freedom, even though uncertainty about their fate dampened that feeling as well. Yehuda and his cousin decided to stay at the family's home in the destroyed ghetto until the Soviet occupation. The community-owned building where the Kleins had lived had a cellar for storing wine. Yehuda and Wolf chose to hide there for the duration of the holy day.

They got there a few hours before the beginning of the fast. Their only food was a slice of bread. They shared part of it for their pre-fast meal, and saved the rest for after the fast. They found other Jews and thus were able to pray with a minyan in the dank cellar. They had one machzor from which one of the worshippers would read aloud, with the rest listening and responding. Among the worshippers were Jews who had lost parents, children, spouses, and siblings. Yehuda was gripped by a powerful storm of emotions during those prayers: he began to realise the impossibility of basing one's service of God solely on the recognition of God's goodness and kindness. It became clear to him that a Jew who lost his wife and children is unable to base his worship of God on gratitude alone. "For the generation that experienced the greatest destruction in Jewish history," he would later explain to his students, "love of God could be based only on faith that stands strong even during a time of hester panim, 'concealment' of God's face. As Job said (13:15): 'Though He may slay me, in Him I trust.'"

Another insight that coalesced in Yehuda's mind during his prayers in the midst of the Holocaust related to reciting the blessing "she-lo asani goy" ("Who has not made me a gentile") during the daily morning prayers. He never recited "she-lo asani goy" with fervour like he did at that time. Despite all the suffering he experienced during that period, Yehuda was proud to belong to the murdered and not the murderers; to the persecuted and not the persecutors.

Despite all the suffering he experienced during that period, Yehuda was proud to belong to the murdered and not the murderers; to the persecuted and not the persecutors.

Yom Kippur ended and the leftover bread failed to alleviate the hunger of Yehuda and Wolf. The next morning, they were forced to leave their cellar in search of food. They went through the apartments in the building. In Yehuda's parents' apartment, they found a piece of bread covered in a layer of green mould and rejoiced as if they had found a treasure. They brushed off the mould, divided the bread, recited the blessings, and ate. Years later, every time Yehuda would notice bread left over at the end of a meal, he would immediately begin calculating how many days it is possible to survive on such a quantity of bread.

But before they could finish eating the mouldy slice, they heard the gate burst open and shouts ascending from the street. The shouts were addressed to them; they were being called to exit the building. As at other moments of danger, Yehuda did not believe in running away this time, either. He intended to hand himself over to them. "We have no reason to stay here," he told Wolf. But Wolf vehemently opposed giving themselves up, and Yehuda acceded.

They hid in one of the rooms of the apartment. Yehuda the pessimist began saying his deathbed confessions. Wolf, hoping to be saved, recited chapters of Psalms. The Hungarian police officers broke down the door to the apartment and entered. They passed through the foyer, surveyed the kitchen and two other rooms, and left the way they came. Wolf and Yehuda breathed sighs of relief. Later they learned that the danger was not a great as they thought. Due to a temporary retreat of Soviet forces, the Hungarian commanders decided to reinstate the work of Jewish prisoners, and to that end they combed the streets of the ghetto in search of labourers. True to his approach that work would stave off death, Yehuda returned with his cousin to the labour camp. Together with one hundred and fifty other prisoners, they were put to work digging defensive trenches in anticipation of the Soviet invasion....

... Just before Chanukah, 5705 (1944), a path to Eretz Yisrael opened. Yehuda sailed from Bucharest, via the Black Sea, to Istanbul, Turkey. He obtained a certificate there and traveled by train, via Syria and Lebanon, to Palestine. He lit the first Chanukah candle in his rail car on Syrian soil, but lit the second candle in Eretz Yisrael. After long months of suffering and travail, he reached Eretz Yisrael on 26 Kislev, 5705.

Until he reached Eretz Yisrael, he did not see his rescue as a complete salvation.

Until he reached Eretz Yisrael, he did not see his rescue as a complete salvation. The dangers he faced even after his liberation from the labor camp showed him that only aliya to Eretz Yisrael would constitute a true rescue. Even after he started a family and decided to commemorate his survival each year with a family thanksgiving meal, he chose not to commemorate the day that Hungary was liberated from the Germans, and not the day that he escaped its soil, but the day he arrived in Palestine.

But there was another reason that he refrained from marking the date of his rescue: he was always bothered by the question of why he survived. "Was I saved because God selected me and rescued me from the Holocaust," he wondered in his students' presence, "or was it a time of hester panim, during which – according to the Ramban (Rabbi Moshe ben Nachman 1194-1270) – God leaves His people to random chance, and I was saved by chance?" These questions never stopped bothering him. Therefore, he did not declare a personal holiday to mark his rescue, but rather celebrated his salvation together with his arrival in Eretz Yisrael.

The fact that he survived infused Yehuda with a sense of responsibility. He felt that he was obligated to redouble his efforts to replace those who were not fortunate enough to survive. He claimed that his survival gave him the courage to do things that would naturally have been beyond his individual ability.

SHOFAR

תקיעת שופר

(i) The blowing of the shofar, usually and preferably a ram's horn, is the central mitzva (commandment) of Rosh Hashana. At least 30 notes of three basic types – tekia, shevarim, teruah – must be blown, in the sequence set out below. Additional notes are blown to accompany the Musaf prayers, whose themes relate to the Shofar. The Shofar is not blown on Shabbat.

תקיעה	שברים תרועה	תקיעה
תקיעה	שברים תרועה	תקיעה
תקיעה	שברים תרועה	תקיעה
תקיעה	שברים	תקיעה
תקיעה	שברים	תקיעה
תקיעה	שברים	תקיעה
תקיעה	תרועה	תקיעה
תקיעה	תרועה	תקיעה
תקיעה גדולה	תרועה	תקיעה

How are you going to hear the shofar this year? Why do you think Jews have gone to such lengths to listen to the Shofar? What does the Shofar tell you about sound as an expression of being Jewish, alongside words?

The Shofar

Dayan Ivan Binstock

This sermon was delivered by Dayan Ivan Binstock at St John's Wood Synagogue, first day of Rosh Hashana, 2016, a few days after the death of Shimon Peres, the former President and Prime Minister of Israel. During his sermon, Dayan Binstock displayed the silver-plated shofar that Shimon Peres presented to the community on the occasion of his visit to St John's Wood Synagogue in 2009.

The Shofar we have just sounded reminds us of many things. It recalls the binding of Isaac, when God told Abraham to stop and offer up, instead, a ram that had been caught by its horn in a bush. It reminds us of the Torah, given at Mount Sinai, when "the whole mountain trembled violently, and the sound of the shofar grew louder and louder."

It was blown to mark the Jubilee, the 50th year, when freedom was proclaimed throughout the land.

The shofar was the sound of victory at Jericho.

It was blown in celebration when King David brought the Ark to Jerusalem.

Jeremiah calls it the sound of war.

Amos called it the sound of danger: "When the shofar sounds in a city, do not the people tremble?"

Joel called it the sound of the "End of Days."

One of the psalms we say on Friday night calls it the herald proclaiming the arrival of the King: "With trumpets and the blast of the shofar, shout for joy before the Lord, the King."

There is another association, particular to this synagogue, at this particular time that the shofar represents.

In 2009, Shimon Peres as President of the State of Israel visited the UK. He addressed a public meeting at this synagogue. The shul was packed to capacity – even more people than here today. I had the honour of welcoming the President. Then, before he spoke, he presented me the gift of this shofar, to accept on behalf of the community as a memento of his visit.

The inscription on the stand reads:

Presented by Shimon Peres, President of the State of Israel.

As it is silver-plated I will not blow it on Rosh Hashana since it is invalid for the mitzva of blowing the shofar, but I plan to blow it, please God, at the

The shofar presented by Shimon Peres

end of Yom Kippur when it may be used to mark the culmination of that day.

Looking back at the life of this outstanding leader of Israel and the Jewish people, it was in retrospect a deeply symbolic gift from a man who, in many ways, was symbolised by a shofar.

If the shofar recalls sacrifice Shimon Peres made enormous sacrifices for his people.

If the shofar reminds us of the bond we forged at Sinai, then Shimon Peres was a proud Jew who never forgot the words, as President Obama reminded us of in his eulogy, that were said when Shimon Peres parted from his grandfather in Poland to leave for Israel: "Shimon, stay a Jew!"

If the shofar reminds us to be alert to danger and the possibility of war, Shimon Peres understood that very well. His vision and foresight laid the foundation of Israel's formidable armed forces.

If the shofar reminds us military victory, as relating to the biblical Jericho when conquered by Joshua, then Shimon duly deserved the credit for his contribution to those victories.

If the shofar celebrates the centrality of Jerusalem, then Shimon, who upheld the importance of Jerusalem in any future peace settlement, is fittingly buried within its borders.

If the shofar proclaims the arrival of a leader, then Shimon Peres as Prime

Minister, President, elder statesman par excellence, gave lustre to his office.

And, if the shofar urges us to yearn for era of peace for Israel and mankind, then Shimon never ceased from proclaiming this call.

For those of you who are Hebrew speakers and appreciate wordplay, you may like to know that 'Shimon Peres' in Hebrew is an anagram of Shofar Menusa "שופר מנוסע" "The travelled Shofar".

May this great man who symbolised so many dimensions of the Shofar during his lifetime, be a source of blessing and inspiration to us all. Amen!

But here we are, us lesser mortals on Rosh Hashana, with our own shofar and the meaning that sound has for us.

If the shofar celebrates the centrality of Jerusalem, then Shimon, who upheld the importance of Jerusalem in any future peace settlement, is fittingly buried within its borders.

I think the significance given to the shofar by our great rabbi and leader of the middle ages, Moses Maimonides (often referred to by acronym as the 'Rambam'), is the one most appropriate for our times.

Maimonides calls the shofar of Rosh Hashana a wake-up call. He says that without such a call, we can sleepwalk through life, caring about trivialities. The sound of the shofar wakes us up and makes us conscious of the fragility of life.

Who knows how much time we have left? None of us will live forever.

So how do we use our time?

The shofar is challenging with the simple, basic question: Who am I?

What are the most important things in my life?

What do I want to be remembered for? If, as a purely hypothetical exercise, we were to imagine reading our own obituary, what would we want it to say?

These are the questions Rosh Hashana urges us to ask ourselves. As we pray to God to write us in the book of life, God asks us what we intend to do with this, His most precious gift.

How do we use our time?

Much recent research on happiness yields surprising conclusions. We can spend our days in pursuit of wealth, yet beyond a certain comfort zone where we do not have to worry, greater wealth is not correlated with higher levels of happiness. The status of a particular job has less to do with happiness than the fulfilment we receive from a job well done.

The sources of happiness lie all around us: our family, our friends, the work we do voluntarily, the sense we have of being part of a community,

Shimon Peres

the feeling we have that we are part of something worthwhile.

A whole series of medical research projects has shown that faith, prayer and regular attendance at a house of worship actually have an effect on health and life expectancy. Not always, for surely we all know of deeply spiritual people who die tragically young. But for the most part, faith gives us an anchor in the storm, a compass as we navigate the future, a shelter when we are buffeted by the winds of circumstance.

Often in the highly charged debates between atheists and religious believers, it seems as if all religion is, is a set of beliefs. It surely is, but that is not all it is. Judaism is a way of life, a code of conduct, a calendar. It shapes our experience of time into a kind of rhythm. Three times daily prayer, Shabbat, the festivals and the Days of Awe (Rosh Hashana and Yom Kippur) function like paragraph- and chapter-breaks in the story of our lives.

So we work, but one day in seven we also rest and spend more time than usual with family and friends. In shul we re-establish our links with the community. Through the festivals we relive the history of our people, and cure ourselves of the narrow sense of living for the moment. On Rosh Hashana we ask, "Why am I here?" On Yom Kippur we try to make amends for the wrongs we have done, and rededicate ourselves to the things we hold holy.

Does a purely secular lifestyle offer a greater chance of happiness?

One of the most extraordinary scientific findings of all is that in the space of two generations, as people in the West have grown more affluent, so have they grown less happy. Depression and stress-related syndromes have all risen between 300 and 1,000 percent. The phenomenon has a name: affluenza. The consumer society is built on making us want what we do not yet have. Judaism is predicated on celebrating what we do have.

I know it is a well-worn cliché, but no one's last thought was, "I wish I had spent more time in the office." Almost no one's obituary praises him or her for the car they drove, the clothes they wore, the homes they built, or the holidays they took. These things are not unimportant, but they are externalities. They are about what we own, not who we are. They give us short-term pleasure, not long-term fulfilment.

That is what Maimonides was talking about when he spoke about the shofar of Rosh Hashana. It is God's call to us.

We may not be able to aspire to achievements as far-reaching as Shimon Peres but we are still challenged by our shofar.

Where are you?

What are you doing with your life?

Do you care about the things that have value but not a price?

Do you spend your time on the important, or only on the urgent?

Judaism is full of details. As a great architect once said, "God is in the details." But the details are brushstrokes in a magnificent painting that we can only appreciate if we step back and look at it as a whole.

In the year to come, what will you live for? Will you listen to your wake-up call?

Judaism turns life into a work of art. It consecrates our love for our dear ones. It sanctifies our most physical acts, through the laws of kashrut and taharat hamishpacha. It engages our hearts in prayer, our minds in study. It asks us, through the laws of tzedaka, to look on our possessions as things God has entrusted into our safekeeping, with the condition that we share some of what we have with those who have less.

Chesed – the love that is kindness – binds our communities into networks of support for people experiencing crisis, illness or bereavement. Jewish faith tells us that we are not alone in the universe, that at the heart of being is One who created us in love, hears our prayers, and believes in us more than we believe in ourselves.

As the sounds of the shofar now fade away, I ask you, in my name, in Shimon Peres' name, in the name of our people and in the name of our God: In the year to come, what will you live for? Will you listen to your wake-up call? We will always fall short of our highest ideals; everyone does. But we stand as tall as the values that inspire us.

May God write you, your family and all Israel in the Book of Life with a year of blessing for us and the whole world.

UNTANEH TOKEF

וּנְתַנֶּה תֹּקֶף

ⓘ   This dramatic prayer about the start of the year as a time of judgement is a central part of the Chazan's public rendition of the Musaf prayers. Portraying God as our shepherd and us as His sheep, it ends with the dramatic statement that 'teshuva, tefilla and tzedaka' - 'repentance, prayer and charity avert the evil of the decree'.

בְּרֹאשׁ הַשָּׁנָה On Rosh HaShana it is written / and on Yom Kippur it is sealed: / how many will pass away and how many will be born; / who will live and who will die; / who in his due time and who before; / who by water and who by fire; / who by sword and who by beast; / who of hunger and who of thirst; / who by earthquake and who by plague; / who by strangling and who by stoning; / who will rest and who will wander; / who will be calm and who will be harassed; / who will be at ease and who will suffer; / who will become poor and who will grow rich; / who cast down and who raised high.

בְּרֹאשׁ הַשָּׁנָה יִכָּתֵבוּן / וּבְיוֹם צוֹם כִּפּוּר יֵחָתֵמוּן.
כַּמָּה יַעַבְרוּן וְכַמָּה יִבָּרֵאוּן
מִי יִחְיֶה וּמִי יָמוּת / מִי בְקִצּוֹ וּמִי לֹא בְקִצּוֹ
מִי בַמַּיִם וּמִי בָאֵשׁ / מִי בַחֶרֶב וּמִי בַחַיָּה / מִי בָרָעָב וּמִי בַצָּמָא
מִי בָרַעַשׁ וּמִי בַמַּגֵּפָה / מִי בַחֲנִיקָה וּמִי בַסְּקִילָה.
מִי יָנוּחַ וּמִי יָנוּעַ / *מִי יִשָּׁקֵט וּמִי יִטָּרֵף
מִי יִשָּׁלֵו וּמִי יִתְיַסָּר / מִי יֵעָנִי וּמִי יֵעָשֵׁר / מִי יִשָּׁפֵל וּמִי יָרוּם.

FASTING   CRYING   GIVING
But REPENTANCE, PRAYER and CHARITY
avert the evil of the decree.

צוֹם   קוֹל   מָמוֹן
וּתְשׁוּבָה וּתְפִלָּה וּצְדָקָה / מַעֲבִירִין אֶת רֹעַ הַגְּזֵרָה.

Why are 'teshuva, tefilla and tzedaka' keys to a successful Yamim Noraim? What do they challenge you to do?

Getting the Reward you Deserve

Dr Daniel Rose

LouAnne Johnson was a retired U.S. Marine who decided to become a teacher as a second career. But she soon found the job was more of a challenge than she could have ever imagined. When she arrived on her first day, she found she would be teaching of a group of tough, hostile teenagers from underprivileged backgrounds. Many of her students were involved in gang warfare and drug-dealing. Not one was motivated to learn, and they all refused to cooperate or listen to her at all.

LouAnne was desperate to reach the students and make a difference in their lives, and tried to persuade them to learn in numerous ways, including using contemporary music, teaching them karate, and using themes and language of the street, helping her students to connect their reality to the subjects they were studying. She even rewarded their efforts with candy bars, reward incentives, and a trip to a theme park (much to the anger of the school authorities!). These creative approaches had various degrees of success, but she finally found the secret to motivate her students when she had the idea to give each of them an A grade for the whole year at the beginning of the semester! She told them that she believed deep down that each of them deserved the A, and had the potential to achieve it, and it was there for the taking. Now all they had to do was maintain it by working hard throughout the year! Sometimes being given something in reward is less effective at motivating us than the threat of losing something!

Sometimes being given something in reward is less effective at motivating us than the threat of losing something!

(From Rabbi Sacks' Covenant & Conversation Family Edition, Behar-Bechukotai 5780/2020)

The Courage to Grow – A Message for Yom Kippur

Rabbi Lord Sacks

I vividly remember the surprise and delight I had when I first read Jane Austen's 'Emma'. It was the first time I had read a novel in which you see a character changing over time. Emma is an intelligent young woman who believes she understands other people better than they do. So she sets about arranging their lives – she is an English "shadchan", matchmaker – with disastrous consequences, because not only does she not understand others; she does not even understand herself. By the end of the novel, though, she is a different person: older, wiser and humbler. Of course, since this is a Jane Austen story, it ends happily ever after.

In the more than 50 years that have passed since I read the book, one question has fascinated me. Where did Western civilisation get the idea that people can change? It is not an obvious idea. Many great cultures have simply not thought in these terms. The Greeks, for instance, believed that we are what we are, and we cannot change

The more I studied and researched, the more I realised that Judaism was the first system in the world to develop a clear sense of human free will.

what we are. They believed that character is destiny, and the character itself is something we are born with, although it may take great courage to realise our potential. Heroes are born, not made. Plato believed that some human beings were gold, others silver, and others bronze. Aristotle believed that some are born to rule, and others to be ruled. Before the birth of Oedipus, his fate and that of his father, Laius, have already been foretold by the Delphic Oracle, and nothing they can do will avert it.

This is precisely the opposite of the key sentence we say on Rosh Hashana and Yom Kippur, that "Teshuva (repentance), tefilla (prayer) and tzedaka (charity) avert the evil decree." That is what happened to the inhabitants of Nineveh in the story we read at Mincha on Yom Kippur. There was a decree: "In forty days Nineveh will be destroyed." But the people of Nineveh repent, and the decree is cancelled. There is no fate that is final, no diagnosis without a second opinion – half of Jewish jokes are based on this idea.

The more I studied and researched, the more I realised that Judaism was the first system in the world to develop a clear sense of human free will. As

Isaac Bashevis Singer (1902-1991), who was awarded the Nobel Prize for Literature in 1978, wittily put it, "We have to be free; we have no choice."

This is the idea at the heart of Teshuva. It is not just confession, not just saying "Al chet shechatanu", for the sins we have committed. It is not just remorse: "Ashamnu", we have sinned. It is the determination to change, the decision that I am going to learn from my mistakes, that I am going to act differently in future, that I am determined to become a different kind of person.

To paraphrase Rabbi Joseph B. Soloveitchik (1903-1993) of Yeshiva University in New York, to be a Jew is to be creative, and our greatest creation is our self. As a result, more than 3000 years before Jane Austen, we see in Torah and in Tanach, the Hebrew Bible, a process in which people change.

To take an obvious example: Moses. We see him at the start of his mission as a man who cannot speak easily or fluently. "I am not a man of words." "I am slow of speech and tongue." "I have uncircumcised lips." But by the end he is the most eloquent and visionary of all the prophets. Moses changed.

Domenico Fetti, The Triumph of Elijah over the Prophets of Baal, c. 1622

One of the most fascinating contrasts is between two Biblical characters who were often thought to resemble one another, indeed were sometimes identified as the same person in two incarnations: Pinchas and Elijah. Both were zealots. But Pinchas changed. God gave him a covenant of peace and he became a man of peace. We see him in later life (the Book of Joshua ch.22) leading a peace negotiation between the rest of the Israelites and the tribes of Reuben, Gad and part of Menasseh who had settled on the far side of the Jordan, a mission successfully accomplished.

Elijah was no less a zealot than Pinchas. Yet there is a remarkable scene sometime after his great confrontation with the prophets of Baal at Mount Carmel. He is at Mount Horeb, another name for Mount Sinai. God asks him, "What are you doing here, Elijah?" Elijah replies, "I have been very zealous for the Lord God Almighty." God then sends a whirlwind, shaking mountain and shattering rocks, but God was not in the wind. Then God sends an earthquake, but God was not in the earthquake. Then God sends fire, but God was not in the fire. Then God speaks in a "kol demamah dakah", a still small voice. He asks Elijah the same question again, "What are you doing here, Elijah?" and Elijah replies in exactly the same words as he had done before: "I have been very zealous for the Lord God Almighty." At that point God tells Elijah to appoint Elisha as his successor (1 Kings 19).

Elijah has not changed. He has not understood that God now wants him to exercise a different kind of leadership, defending Israel not criticising it, as the great commentator

Jill Bolte Taylor

Rashi explains. He is asking Elijah to make a similar transformation to the one Pinchas made when he became a man of peace, but Elijah, unlike Pinchas, did not change. Even his words do not change, despite the momentous vision. He had become too holy for this world, so God took him to heaven in a chariot of fire.

It was Judaism, through the concept of Teshuva, that brought into the world the idea that we can change. We are not predestined to continue to be what we are. Even today, this remains a radical idea. Many biologists and neuroscientists believe that our character and actions are wholly determined by our genes, our DNA. Choice, character change, and free will, are – they say – illusions.

They are wrong. One of the great discoveries of recent years has been the scientific demonstration of the plasticity of the brain. The most dramatic example of this is the case of Jill Bolte Taylor. In 1996, aged 37, she suffered a massive stroke that completely destroyed the functioning of the left hemisphere of her brain. She could not walk, talk, read, write, or even recall the details of her life. But she was very unusual in one respect. She was a Harvard neuroscientist. As a result, she was able to realise precisely what had happened to her.

For eight years she worked every day, together with her mother, to exercise her brain. By the end, she had recovered all her faculties, using her right hemisphere to develop the skills normally exercised by the left brain. You can read her story in her book, 'My Stroke of Insight', or see her deliver a TED lecture on the subject. Taylor is only the most dramatic example of what is becoming clearer each year: that by an effort of will, we can change not just our behaviour, not just our emotions, nor even just our character, but the very structure and architecture of our brain. Rarely was there a more dramatic scientific vindication of the great Jewish insight that we can change.

That is the challenge of Teshuva.

There are two kinds of problem in life: technical and adaptive. When you face the first, you go to an expert for the solution. You are feeling ill, you go to the doctor, who diagnoses the illness and prescribes a pill. That is a technical problem. The second kind is where we ourselves are the problem. We go to the doctor, he listens carefully, does various tests, and then says: "I can prescribe a pill, but in the long term, it is not going to help. You are overweight, under-exercised and overstressed. If you don't change your lifestyle, all the pills in the world will not help." That is an adaptive problem.

May this year be the start of a new life for each of us. Let us have the courage to grow.

Adaptive problems call for Teshuva, and Teshuva itself is premised on the proposition that we can change. All too often we tell ourselves we cannot. We are too old, too set in our ways. It is too much trouble. When we do that, we deprive ourselves of God's greatest gift to us: the ability to change. This was one of Judaism's greatest gifts to Western civilisation.

It is also God's call to us on Yom Kippur. This is the time when we ask ourselves where have we gone wrong? Where have we failed? When we tell ourselves the answer, that is when we need the courage to change. If we believe we cannot, we will not. If we believe we can, we may.

The great question Yom Kippur poses to us is: Will we grow in our Judaism, our emotional maturity, our knowledge, our sensitivity, or will we stay what we were? Never believe we cannot be different, greater, more confident, more generous, more understanding and forgiving than we were. May this year be the start of a new life for each of us. Let us have the courage to grow.

TASHLICH

(i) A brief ceremony, with prayers recited in view of water as an expression of our desire that God 'wash away' our sins. Held on the first afternoon of Rosh Hashana unless that day is Shabbat in which case Tashlich is postponed until the following day.

מִי־אֵל כָּמְוֹךָ Who, God is like You,
who pardons iniquity and forgives the transgression
of the remnant of His heritage?
He does not stay angry for ever,
but delights in loving-kindness.
He will again have compassion on us, suppress our iniquities,
and cast into the depths of the sea all their sins.
Grant truth to Jacob, kindness to Abraham,
as You promised our fathers in days long ago.

מִי־אֵל כָּמְוֹךָ
נֹשֵׂא עָוֹן וְעֹבֵר עַל פֶּשַׁע לִשְׁאֵרִית נַחֲלָתוֹ
לֹא הֶחֱזִיק לָעַד אַפּוֹ
כִּי חָפֵץ חֶסֶד הוּא:
יָשׁוּב יְרַחֲמֵנוּ יִכְבֹּשׁ עֲוֺנֹתֵינוּ
וְתַשְׁלִיךְ בִּמְצֻלוֹת יָם כָּל־חַטֹּאתָם:
תִּתֵּן אֱמֶת לְיַעֲקֹב חֶסֶד לְאַבְרָהָם
אֲשֶׁר נִשְׁבַּעְתָּ לַאֲבֹתֵינוּ מִימֵי קֶדֶם:

What are we asking God for in Tashlich and why? What does the fact that God 'does not stay angry for ever' teach us? Look at the article on the next page. How can we prevent sins of 'fake news'?

Living in the Era of Fake News

Sivan Rahav Meir

Yesterday someone attached my name to text that I did not compose. The text was a frightening scenario of what could happen in Israel due to the coronavirus. This text was sent to me more than 100 times with reactions that ranged from "Powerful!" to "You really wrote this?".

It's a strange feeling. You know you didn't write it but you have no control over it and there is nothing you can do about it. You only know that at this very moment it is being shared in more and more groups and every moment brings another greeting from someone who saw it. It says that someone who quotes the words of another in that person's name brings redemption to the world. What do we say about someone who does exactly the opposite?

This was not serious fake news, no real damage was done, but I thought about more problematic fake news that's running around these days. How many recommendations from "doctors", how many letters from "experts", how many alarming and unverified reports are being broadcast over media networks without anyone stopping to check their reliability? These reports are copied and shared with the words "No way!" or "Is this true?" added on. But if you don't know if something is true, why copy and share it just to put other people under stress?

The Chafetz Chaim said that speaking Lashon Hara (evil speech) is like tearing a pillow in the town square when the feathers fly in every direction. How much more perilous is speech that is utterly false yet flies much further than feathers thanks to instantaneous communication to every corner of the earth in the digital new media era.

Reality is confusing enough. Don't make it even more confusing.

KOL NIDREI

כָּל נִדְרֵי

(i) The opening part of the Yom Kippur service.

כָּל נִדְרֵי

וֶאֱסָרֵי וַחֲרָמֵי וְקוֹנָמֵי וְכִנּוּיֵי וְקִנּוּסֵי וּשְׁבוּעוֹת
דִּנְדַרְנָא, וּדְאִשְׁתַּבַּעְנָא, וּדְאַחֲרִימְנָא וּדְאָסַרְנָא עַל נַפְשָׁתָנָא
מִיּוֹם כִּפּוּרִים זֶה עַד יוֹם כִּפּוּרִים הַבָּא עָלֵינוּ לְטוֹבָה.
בְּכֻלְּהוֹן אִחֲרַטְנָא בְהוֹן, כֻּלְּהוֹן יְהוֹן שָׁרָן.
שְׁבִיקִין, שְׁבִיתִין, בְּטֵלִין וּמְבֻטָּלִין
לָא שְׁרִירִין, וְלָא קַיָּמִין.
נִדְרָנָא לָא נִדְרֵי
וֶאֱסָרָנָא לָא אֱסָרֵי
וּשְׁבוּעָתָנָא לָא שְׁבוּעוֹת.

EVERY VOW
and bind, ban, restriction,
every term that sets things out of bounds,
every penalty and oath;
all that we vow or swear, ban or bar from ourselves,
from this Yom Kippur until that which is to come –
let it be for the good –
each one, we regret. Let each be released,
forgotten, halted, null and void,
without power and without hold.
What we vow is not vowed,
what we bind is not bound,
and what we swear is not sworn.

Can you really change a vow? If so, how? Does Kol Nidre
'work' or is it a wake-up call? Why has this prayer and service
captured the Jewish imagination over the generations? If you
are not at shul, how will your home look for Kol Nidrei?

Kol Nidrei and The Long Road to Peace

Naftali Lau-Lavie

Naftali Lau-Lavie (1928-2014) was a renowned Israeli journalist and diplomat, who miraculously survived the Holocaust along with his younger brother (later to become Rabbi Yisrael Meir Lau). In this adapted extract from his moving autobiography "Balaam's Prophecy", he describes an unusual Kol Nidre night with the then Israeli Foreign Minister Moshe Dayan, ahead of the arduous, lengthy Israel-Egypt peace treaty negotiations.

The hardest part in finalizing the treaty was to commence one month later at Blair House and the Madison Hotel. It took a six-week dialogue to formulate the version of the peace treaty which would be signed at the end of March 1979, and then only after concerted efforts to move the parties from their entrenched positions. At the end of the Camp David summit, President Carter sent congratulatory letters to Sadat and Begin and suggested that the practical discussions of a peace treaty based on the principles of the Camp David "Accords" should begin on October 12 at Blair House in Washington. This was the day after Yom Kippur. We had to arrive two days earlier and observe the fast in the Madison Hotel, a forty-minute walk from the nearest synagogue.

On Tuesday morning, October 10, we arrived in Washington from New York, where Dayan had addressed the UN General Assembly and met foreign ministers and the UN secretary general. Upon arrival in Washington, Dayan was invited for a talk with President Carter and his senior aides, which lasted almost until the beginning of the Yom Kippur fast. We barely managed to gulp down a couple of bites of the pre-fast meal and rushed by car to the Kol Nidrei service at the Kesher Israel Synagogue in Georgetown.

This relatively small synagogue was filled almost beyond capacity – not only by the regular worshipers, but by numerous journalists who had gathered there. Dayan again asked me to sit next to him to help him find the appropriate prayers in the book. When he saw me removing my shoes, he followed suit. When he was honoured by an invitation to open the Holy Ark for one of the prayers, he passed inspection but was unsure of what he was supposed to do. I accompanied him to the Ark, helped him slide open the velvet curtain and open the doors of the Ark, revealing the scrolls of the Torah. At the conclusion of the particular prayer, he confidently closed the doors and curtain of the Ark, and returned to his seat. At the end of the service, Rabbi Philip Rabinowitz rose to bless the important visitors from Israel and wished them success in their endeavor to bring peace to the Jewish people and their land. The congregation was visibly moved; so were we Israeli guests. When we came outside, we saw the procession of black limousines waiting as usual, surrounded by cars of the security details. At the open door of the Dayan limousine, I gave him the traditional

We barely managed to gulp down a couple of bites of the pre-fast meal and rushed by car to the Kol Nidrei service at the Kesher Israel Synagogue in Georgetown.

wish for a gemar chatima tova (may you be sealed in the Book of Life) and an easy fast. We were still shaking hands when he said with a smile, "Yom Kippur obligates me too," and joined us in the long walk to the hotel, with the convoy of limousines and police escorting us at our pace.

Who Will Live and Who Will Die

Rabbi Yechiel Wasserman

I received the emergency call-up to my reserve unit immediately after Yom Kippur. I was part of a tank crew, the signalman and loader in a Centurion tank based in the north of the country. I was told to report to an assembly point at a park in the centre of Jerusalem. I drove to my house, bid farewell to my parents and family, and my father of blessed memory gave me a blessing before I left. Among other things,

Rabbi Wasserman during his IDF service

he told me that "the tefillin that you carry will protect you from any harm."

On Yom Kippur 5734 (1973) I was a sixth-year student at a hesder yeshiva, Yeshivat Hakotel in the Old City of Jerusalem, which combined yeshiva studies with army service. I prayed at the yeshiva together with my friends, teachers, rabbis and many guests and visitors who had come to visit for Yom Kippur since the yeshiva is located near to the Western Wall. The recitation of the dramatic Untaneh Tokef prayer was one of the highlights of the Yom Kippur service, with the hundreds present praying with devotion and a sense of purpose, shedding tears as the voice of the chazan, the leader of the service, rang clear: "Who will live and who will die, who will die at his predestined time and who before his time … who by water and who by fire."

Not one of those present imagined that these words would take on a real, practical significance just a few hours later. In the afternoon, when the alarms began to sound, the rumours began to spread regarding the war and the general call-up. Later in the afternoon, the first students began to leave the yeshiva on their way to their units.

By the end of this holiest of days, most of the students, myself included, were on their way to the front.

Rabbi Wasserman (left with members of his tank unit

When I arrived at my assembly point in the park, hundreds of reservists had already gathered there. Among them were many of my friends from the yeshiva as well as others from my unit. The mood in the Egged bus in which we were driving towards the Sinai Desert was sombre, as news of the hard battles being fought at the front kept streaming in over the radio. Most of the people on the bus sat quietly, deep in thought, looking out of the window wondering if they would return from the war, if they would ever see their families and hometowns again. These thoughts were suddenly interrupted when we arrived at our base. Quickly, we received our personal equipment and began loading the tanks. On Sunday night, the second night of the war, we began travelling south toward the Suez Canal.

All the while, bloody, hard-fought holding battles were being waged along the front lines. In the briefing we received before our departure it became clear to us that the situation was dire and that we, the reservists, must arrive as quickly as possible in order to reinforce the units that were already engaged. By nightfall, we were already in place. Our first shots were fired as

Wounded soldiers receiving treatment

we engaged enemy tanks that blocked our path, and after a difficult battle, the Egyptian unit facing us retreated.

On Tuesday morning we found ourselves near the Bitter Lake in the midst of a pitched battle that continued until after midnight that night. This was October 8, the date of the first attempt at a counterattack in the hope of driving the Egyptian armour back.

It is difficult, and perhaps even impossible, to describe the terrifying scenes of battle, with shells flying through the air and tanks being hit, the screams of the wounded, the horrific sight of the injured and the dead. Several of my friends were killed that harrowing day and a number of others were wounded.

At first light, after a short night's rest, the battalion began preparations for another day of combat.

In the afternoon, after several hours of intense fighting, we captured a hill from which we could see hundreds of Egyptian soldiers and vehicles fleeing south. Soon we heard the command from brigade headquarters: Charge! Fire all available guns. The tanks jumped forward with us standing in the turrets unprotected. However, after several minutes it became clear that we had charged straight into an anti-tank ambush. We took fire from all directions and experienced heavy losses.

The Sagger anti-tank missile, provided to the Egyptians by the Soviet Union and which we experienced for the first time in the war, packs a deadly punch. My tank took a direct hit in the turret from a Sagger missile, shrapnel flew everywhere and I was hit in my upper body. My face was bloodied, my left hand was severely injured and I couldn't see out of my left eye. In

I remembered my tefillin that were in the tank, in a rear equipment compartment, and then I lost consciousness and everything went black.

seconds I felt that I was losing strength. The last image that I remembered was Ezra Bashari, my tank driver, coming up to the turret, extricating me and laying me down next to the tank, which in the meantime had gone up in flames. I remembered my tefillin that were in the tank, in a rear equipment compartment, and then I lost consciousness and everything went black.

Later, my friends told me that I had run to the equipment compartment, grabbed my tefillin and run away as best as I could before collapsing. They explained that I was soon lifted up and placed in the turret of the adjacent, retreating tank.

While the tank made its way to the road, a medical team began treating me and I was taken by helicopter to an emergency field hospital in Refidim, a large base in the Sinai. From there I was flown with other wounded soldiers, still unconscious, to Tel Hashomer hospital near Tel Aviv.

I am filled with appreciation for the person who helped make that period less painful and who gave me much encouragement - Rena Feir, then my fiancée, today my wife...

Several days later, when I regained consciousness and I awoke, I asked the nurse for the time. I had not been able to put on my tefillin on the previous days and I did not want to miss another day. She smiled, told me that I was in a hospital and that I didn't have any tefillin with me. The hospital chaplain brought me a different set of tefillin and I immediately put them on, right there in my hospital bed. I remained in the hospital for several months. I was operated on six times and among other things, I received a cornea transplant (an unusual procedure in those days).

When I look back at my lengthy stay in the hospital, which included multiple surgeries, I am filled with appreciation for the person who helped make that period less painful and who gave me much encouragement - Rena Feir, then my fiancée, today my wife and mother of my three children. Her support and undying optimism, coupled with my desire to regain my strength, rehabilitate myself and start a family, helped to speed the healing process.

On one of the days during my lengthy hospital stay, Rabbi Yisrael Klein, then a student at Yeshivat Kerem Beyavneh and a member of my tank battalion who had fought with me at the Small Bitter Lake near the Suez Canal, came to visit and, to my astonished delight, brought my tefillin!

It was then that I discovered that when I was wounded and moved to the road, the tefillin that had been in my hand fell into the depths of the retreating tank in which I was evacuated, all the way to the floor. On one of the days following the ceasefire, as the crew was cleaning the tank, they found my tefillin inside their pouch, on which I had my full name embroidered. One of my friends from the yeshiva recognised my name, remembering that at the beginning of the war I had received medical treatment on the turret of the tank and that the tefillin had fallen in.

Over 40 years have passed since that terrible war, yet my body still bears the scars of battle. I left the battlefield physically injured but whole in soul and spirit. Many

The Wasserman family at the IDF Armoured Corps Museum, Latrun, Israel. The tank is the same model as Rabbi Wasserman's in 1973.

times, the horrific images of war pass before my eyes, the burnt out tanks and blackened vehicles, the dead and the wounded crying for help.

Ever since the Yom Kippur War, the Untaneh Tokef prayer has taken on special significance for me, as the words "who will live and who will die" received real-life meaning. The person who stands in prayer is helpless before Almighty God. We are "created from dust and shall return to dust." God is the eternal King while Man is akin to "broken clay, a wilted plant, the dust in the wind and the floating dream," forever at God's mercy.

The beauty of the Untaneh Tokef prayer is in its clear and simple presentation of things that became real and tangible on the battlefields of war. In the age of technology, modern people may feel that they are all-powerful. However, even though we can travel in space, create revolutionary and elaborate technologies that allow for intercontinental communication, launch ballistic missiles and spacecraft and to create disease-ending drugs, we still cannot not predict what will happen tomorrow. Everything can change from minute to minute and our worst nightmares may become reality at any given moment. Thus, we still feel that we are governed by God and truly "like pottery in the hand of the craftsman."

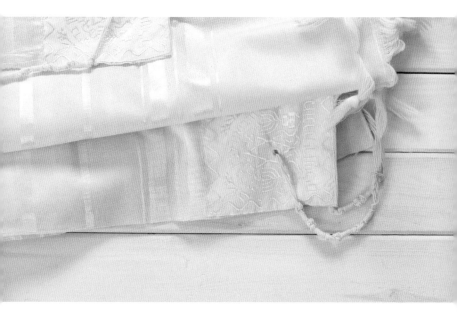

CONFESSION

וִידּוּי

 The "Vidu'i", confessional prayers, are recited on Yom Kippur as part of our requests for God to wipe away our sins.

אָשַׁמְנוּ We have sinned, we have acted treacherously, we have robbed, we have spoken slander.
We have acted perversely, we have acted wickedly, we have acted presumptuously, we have been violent, we have framed lies.
We have given bad advice, we have deceived, we have scorned, we have rebelled, we have provoked, we have turned away, we have committed iniquity, we have transgressed, we have persecuted, we have been obstinate.
We have acted wickedly, we have corrupted, we have acted abominably, we have strayed, we have led others astray.

אָשַׁמְנוּ, בָּגַדְנוּ, גָּזַלְנוּ, דִּבַּרְנוּ דֹּפִי
הֶעֱוִינוּ, וְהִרְשַׁעְנוּ, זַדְנוּ, חָמַסְנוּ, טָפַלְנוּ שֶׁקֶר
יָעַצְנוּ רָע, כִּזַּבְנוּ, לַצְנוּ, מָרַדְנוּ, נִאַצְנוּ, סָרַרְנוּ
עָוִינוּ, פָּשַׁעְנוּ, צָרַרְנוּ, קִשִּׁינוּ עֹרֶף
רָשַׁעְנוּ, שִׁחַתְנוּ, תִּעַבְנוּ, תָּעִינוּ, תִּעְתָּעְנוּ.

What is repentance? Is it a prayer at all, in the way that you would normally understand prayer? Why is Yom Kippur not called a day of repentance, but instead a Day of Atonement?

Fear of Failure?
Fear of Success!

Sivan Rahav Meir

We are afraid to fail although, in fact, we are also afraid to succeed. The famous Jewish-American psychologist Abraham Maslow called this the "Jonah complex". Jonah the prophet fled from his mission in life, from the command to go to the city of Nineveh. He ran away simply in order not to realise his potential.

There are commentators who explain that's what happens in the Torah when twelve spies were sent after the Exodus from the desert to the Land of Israel. Only two choose to explain what they see in an optimistic and empowering way and proclaim that it would be worthwhile to continue on the journey. Ten spies announce that there is no possibility of success and it would be preferable to remain in the desert.

What happened to them? Indeed, it was scary to enter the Land of Israel and to realise our purpose. It was an awesome task that carried a message for the entire world. As Professor Maslow explains, it is easier for us sometimes to repress the positive forces within us. Simply to run away from growth and greatness into our comfort zone.

Even today we are likely to sin with the sin of the spies – in our personal and national lives - and fail to realise any great vision, the very dream of all the generations that came before us. We may rather "remain in the desert" instead of going beyond ourselves.

THE SHEMA

שְׁמַע

(i)   The central statement of Jewish faith, recited in morning and evening prayers daily. The second line is said aloud only on Yom Kippur.

Listen, Israel: the LORD is our God,
the LORD is One.

Aloud: Blessed be the name of His glorious kingdom
for ever and all time.

וְאָהַבְתָּ Love the LORD your God with all your heart, with all your soul, and with all your might. These words which I command you today shall be on your heart. Teach them repeatedly to your children, speaking of them when you sit at home and when you travel on the way, when you lie down and when you rise. Bind them as a sign on your hand, and they shall be an emblem between your eyes. Write them on the doorposts of your house and gates.

שְׁמַע יִשְׂרָאֵל, יהוה אֱלֹהֵינוּ, יהוה ׀ אֶחָד:

בָּרוּךְ שֵׁם כְּבוֹד מַלְכוּתוֹ לְעוֹלָם וָעֶד.

וְאָהַבְתָּ אֵת יהוה אֱלֹהֶיךָ, בְּכָל־לְבָבְךָ וּבְכָל־נַפְשְׁךָ וּבְכָל־מְאֹדֶךָ:
וְהָיוּ הַדְּבָרִים הָאֵלֶּה, אֲשֶׁר אָנֹכִי מְצַוְּךָ הַיּוֹם, עַל־לְבָבֶךָ: וְשִׁנַּנְתָּם
לְבָנֶיךָ וְדִבַּרְתָּ בָּם, בְּשִׁבְתְּךָ בְּבֵיתֶךָ וּבְלֶכְתְּךָ בַדֶּרֶךְ, וּבְשָׁכְבְּךָ
וּבְקוּמֶךָ: וּקְשַׁרְתָּם לְאוֹת עַל־יָדֶךָ וְהָיוּ לְטֹטָפֹת בֵּין עֵינֶיךָ:
וּכְתַבְתָּם עַל־מְזֻזוֹת בֵּיתֶךָ וּבִשְׁעָרֶיךָ:

   Why is this our most fundamental prayer text? Is it a prayer at all as you would normally understand prayer? What does it tell us about being Jewish?

The Shema: Our Acceptance of God as King

The first paragraph of the Shema comes from Moshe's first valedictory speech at the end of the Children of Israel's forty years in the desert, shortly before his death and their entry to the Land of Israel. It is at this final stage of Moshe's life that God instructs him to reinforce acceptance of God, perhaps to show his continuing belief in God, despite his impending death.

The paragraph lists several mitzvot (commandments), such as loving God and having a mezuza on your doorpost. These help us to put the acceptance we declare in the first line of the Shema into practice.

The major themes of the second paragraph, also part of the same valedictory speech, are acceptance of God's mitzvot and reward and punishment. The third paragraph focuses on tzitzit as a reminder for all mitzvot and concludes by remembering the Exodus from Egypt, which we must do morning and evening.

The Shema reaffirms our acceptance of God. We state this belief aloud to encourage us to embrace it as best we can.

At various times, notably during the merciless Roman persecutions in the Land of Israel (such as the Bar Kochba revolt, 133-136 CE) "Shema Yisrael" was the prominent rallying cry of religious belief and Jewish independence.

As such, the Romans tried to ban it, knowing its spiritual power. We revisit this during the Musaf prayers on Yom Kippur when we read the emotional story of the sage Rabbi Akiva, martyred during the Bar Kochba revolt, who recited the Shema and epitomised its lessons even as Roman executioners put him to death.

The Shema reaffirms our acceptance of God. We state this belief aloud to encourage us to embrace it as best we can. We cast our minds back to leaders like Moshe and Rabbi Akiva, learning from their faith both in God and the continuity of Judaism.

Acquittal and Purification

Rabbi Joseph B. Soloveitchik

The abridged extracts below are from the first chapter of 'On Repentance', teachings of the renowned Rabbi Joseph B. Soloveitchik (1903-93) edited by Dr Pinchas Peli, in which Rabbi Soloveitchik addresses the atonement granted by Yom Kippur. They are resonant with the theme of accepting God's Kingship which we proclaim in the Shema and is an essential stage of teshuva (repentance).

Yom Kippur – the Day of Atonement – has a double function. The first is kapparah – acquittal from sin or atonement: "For the virtue of this very day shall acquit you of sin" (Leviticus 16:30). This was expressed in the prayer recited by the High Priest in the Holy Temple: "Please grant acquittal for sins."

The second aspect of Yom Kippur is taharah – catharsis or purification. As it is written: "For the virtue of this very day shall acquit you of sin, to cleanse you…" This, too, was brought out in the Yom Kippur Temple service. The High Priest pronounced to the assembled people: "Before God, be you cleansed."

These two motifs recur repeatedly in all the prayers said on Yom Kippur. "Acquit us… pour cleansing waters upon us…"

… However, sin also has a polluting quality. The Jewish view recognizes a state of "impurity of sin" (tum'at hachet). The entire Bible abounds in references to this idea of self-pollution, contamination, rolling about in the mire of sin.

This impurity makes its mark on the sinner's personality. Sin, as it were, removes the divine halo from man's head, impairing his spiritual integrity. In addition to the frequent appearance of this idea in Scripture and in the homiletical teachings of the Aggadah, we also find many concrete references to the "impurity of sin" in the Halacha (Jewish law).

An Israelite who has transgressed suffers a reversal in his legal status… This does not constitute further punishment but is rather indicative of a change in his personal status. As a result of sin, man is not the same person he was before. Every man is presumed acceptable as a credible witness. Natural truthfulness is, to my way of thinking, an integral part of man's character. The moment a person sins he lessens his own worth, brings himself down and becomes spiritually defective, thus foregoing his former status. Sin deprives man of his natural privileges and unique human attributes. He is subjected to a complete transformation as his original personality departs, and another one replaces it. This is not a form of punishment, or a fine, and is not imposed in a spirit of anger, wrath or vindictiveness. It is a "metaphysical" corruption of the human personality, of the divine image of man.

The moment a person sins he lessens his own worth, brings himself down and becomes spiritually defective...

The communists speak of the commission of "error" and of "deviation," but have no concept of sin. Error carries no implication of metaphysical impurity or of psychic pollution. An "error" is a legal, rational term which must be distinguished from "sin" which harms the inner quality of man and has a deep and far-reaching effect on his being.

Indeed true teshuvah not only achieves kapparah, it should also bring about taharah from tum'ah (spiritual pollution), liberating man from his hardhearted ignorance and insensitivity. Such teshuvah restores man's spiritual viability and rehabilitates him to his original state.

And sometimes it makes man rise to heights he never dreamed he could reach.

From the Tribe Siddur (Koren/NCSY)

It once happened on the battlefield between two warring nations, that Jew faced Jew in mortal combat. As one of the Jewish soldiers ran for cover into a foxhole, the other called out, "Surrender, or I'll shoot." The hiding soldier, quivering in fear, closed his eyes, and crying, recited the familiar words from his childhood, "Shema Yisrael..." As the other soldier heard these words, he responded with surprise and emotion, "Baruch shem kevod malchuto le'olam va'ed." As he laid down his gun he extended a hand to his former enemy and they embraced as brothers.

TORAH READINGS

קריאת התורה

(i) The Torah reading on Yom Kippur morning describes the Avodah, the service of the Kohen Gadol (High Priest) in the Temple on Yom Kippur. The Haftarah, from the closing chapters of Yeshayahu (Isaiah) is a call for social justice and reflections on the real spiritual objectives of a fast day.

The Avodah at O'Hare

Rabbi Dr. Meir Y. Soloveichik

Yerushalayim (Jerusalem); Yom Kippur; 2500 years ago. There is no Kol Nidrei, no kittels, no congregational sermons. No chazanim, no machzorim, not even Untaneh Tokef. All of Israel's eyes are on one man; he is called Kohen Gadol (the High Priest). Jews assemble in awe and anticipation as the Avodah (the sacrificial service) begins. It is the ultimate reality show, with extraordinary stakes. If the sacrifices are performed properly, with appropriate intent, Klal Yisrael (the Jewish people) will be forgiven. If he proves unworthy, he himself could be struck down and the Avodah invalidated. The climax of the Avodah is the Kohen Gadol's entry into the sanctum sanctorum, into the Holy of Holies. Cradling the cup of blood from the sin-offering, the High Priest completes the sacrifice by sprinkling that blood between the twin poles of the Ark of the Covenant. As he sprinkles, he counts, and all those assembled hear his voice emerging from that sacred site: achat, one sprinkle; achat ve-achat, a second one; achat u-shtayim, one and two.

Chicago; any old Tuesday morning, around fifteen years ago. Rabbi Aaron Soloveichik, my grandfather, rises at the crack of dawn and prepares for his weekly flight to New York, where he teaches Torah at Yeshiva University. It is not an unusual commute, with the following critical caveat:

the rabbi is eighty years old and a stroke victim. He can only walk slowly, haltingly, with cane, with one hand shaking behind his back. Every step is painful; every effort excruciating, and accompanied by an agonizing oy! He heads to O'Hare airport, where is greeted behind the ticket counter by Diana, a non-Jew who has developed a love and respect for this elderly rabbi, and even gave the rabbi's wife her home number in order to assist with travel arrangements. The affection is mutual; he calls her "the real princess Diana." He gets his boarding pass, and is wheeled by an attendant towards the gate. Of course he has to be frisked first by security, as he is clearly a potential security threat. Once, in fact, the airport security examined him, and allowed him through, only to call him back so the guard could check under his big black hat, no doubt for the grenades which he could be secreting under there. But he is only packing a Tehillim (Psalms), which he reads on the plane. He arrives in Newark and takes a cab to Washington Heights, to Yeshiva University. Now he has reached the last and most difficult leg of his journey, one more obstacle that has to be confronted before he could reach the shiur (lesson) that mattered so much to him. Yeshiva's main building is a hundred years old, and not accessible, and he has to climb up a staircase. And so he begins to do so, his teeth gritting in pain; and as he pulls himself up each step, he tends to count to himself how many he has climbed; and he utilizes the machzor as his method of counting, muttering to himself the Kohen's mantra: achat, one step; achat ve-achat, another step; achat u-shtayim, another. I remember vividly him counting this way whenever he took the stairs, but it was my father who noted to me that perhaps this was symbolic of something larger; that for my zeidie (grandfather) every day was a day when we had to bring a korban (offering) to Ha-Kadosh Baruch Hu (the Holy One, blessed be He) by sacrificing of our time and energy for Torah. In other words, for him, every act was an Avodah in miniature, every step up those stairs a small sacrifice for God.

For him, every act was an Avodah in miniature, every step up those stairs a small sacrifice for God.

And this explanation, I believe, makes a lot of sense in light of something that I had heard from my grandfather myself. My grandfather knew a man who was always complaining about his mother. What a nudge, the man used to say. My mother always wants me to come visit her, to call her. I don't have time for that, I'm busy, I work hard. Then this mother took terribly ill, and this man quit his job and devoted himself full time to caring for his mother. In considering this case, my grandfather commented that there are certain things for which, when push comes to shove, we are all prepared to make grand sacrifices. But oddly, we are all too reluctant to make smaller, more frequent sacrifices for the same thing which so obviously means so much to us. According to a remarkable, and bizarre, story in the Talmud, the Sages were once asked by the Greek philosophers "Mah ya'aseh adam ve-yichyeh" – "what should a man do, that he should live"? The rabbis replied: "Yamut et atzmo" – "he should kill himself." My grandfather interpreted the gemara as follows: What ought a man do, that he should live? How should he organize his life? Yamut et atzmo. Let him ponder what he is willing to die for, and then let him live every day for that. Who among us would not give our lives for our kids? Who would not willingly make such a sacrifice? But shouldn't we then feel obligated to sacrifice a bit from a busy schedule in order to spend time with them, every day? And what about our faith? If forced to choose, would we not like to believe that we would martyr ourselves for Judaism? But if Judaism is so important to us, if such an extraordinary sacrifice is possible, why are we so often reluctant to make small sacrifices for our Torah and mitzvot during every day of our lives? And so we encounter a rabbi struggling to teach Torah until the day he died; if he was prepared to give his life for the Torah, then he was certainly prepared to live for it, and sacrifice every day to continue teaching Torah.

If Rabbi Akiva, murdered and mutilated by the Romans for his loyalty to Judaism, joyously greeted the opportunity to fulfill the awesome mitzva that is martyrdom, then ought not this rabbi, who, while suffering tremendously, is not forced to sacrifice in similar proportions, ought he not at least joyously number and proclaim his own sacrifices with an achat, achat ve-achat!!

Chicago; October 2001. Soldier Field. Home of the Chicago Bears. A yarmulke-doffing Chicagoan took his seat at a football game. The man next to him notices the skullcap, and asked the Jew if he had a rabbi. Of course, the Jew said. Well, said the non-kippah-wearing man, my wife and I aren't Jewish, but we have a rabbi too: Rabbi Aaron Soloveichik. "Oh," the Jew said casually, "you mean the Rabbi Aaron Soloveichik who just passed away?" The man blanched, and dropped his Coke on the floor. He took out his cell phone, dialed, and said, "Honey, the rabbi has died." The woman on the phone began to cry. Of course this man was the husband of Diana of O'Hare airport, the real princess Diana, who was crying because she would never see her rabbi again. It is true, as a cousin of mine pointed out to me, that God providentially arranged for this wonderful woman's husband to sit next to this member of Chicago's Jewish community, in order that she would be informed of Rabbi Soloveichik's passing, and to allow her to mourn him and honour his memory. But even more interesting is her genuine admiration for this rabbi, and her profound grief now that he was gone. Why did she care

so much in the first place? Diana never observed the Torah he taught, never understood the Talmud he analyzed. What moved her was the notion of a man for whom his faith meant so much that he was willing to make this trip week after week, an eighty-year-old stroke victim who spent each day making sacrifices for what he believed was important.

Yerushalayim; Yom Kippur, 1900 years ago. The Temple lies in ruins. It had for generations been the sole medium by which the Jewish people renewed their relationship with God. Without the Ketoret (incense in the Temple), without the exculpation of Azazel (goat sent to the wilderness), without the achat, achat ve-achat, atonement appeared impossible. And then Rabbi Akiva introduces the following extraordinary idea: Ashrecha Yisrael, fortunate are you O Israel, before whom are you purified, Lifnei Avichem She-Ba-Shamayim, before your Father in Heaven. In the absence of the ability of the High Priest to stand before God, God will stand before each and every one of us. Instead of a Kohen Gadol, each of us atones for ourselves; and instead of one ritual sacrifice, it is we who must resolve to make sacrifices throughout our daily lives, sacrifices of our time for things that matter, that are worth dying for, and certainly worth living for.

We are, all of us, on Yom Kippur, akin to the Kohen Gadol in the Kodesh Ha-Kodashim, the Holy of Holies in the Temple; we gather together as an Am Mamlechet Kohanim, a nation of kingly priests. And it is the Almighty who watches in anxious anticipation to see if our Avodah will be successful, the Ribono Shel Olam (the Master of the Universe) who listens for our own announcement, achat, achat ve-achat, God, I am willing to sacrifice for what is important, God, I realise that there are certain things for which I would give my life, so God, please give me so many more years to live for them.

MAREH KOHEN

מַרְאֵה כֹהֵן

ⓘ This song expresses the joy of the Kohen Gadol (the High Priest) after he successfully concluded his service in the Temple on Yom Kippur.

The Leader:
אֱמֶת Truly how splendid was the High Priest,
as he came out of the Holy of Holies in peace, without harm.

*The following piyut was traditionally recited responsively,
the Leader chanting each line and the congregation responding with
"was the appearance of the [High] Priest." In some
congregations, the whole piyut is sung collectively.*

Like the heavenly canopy stretched out over the angels
was the appearance of the [High] Priest.
Like the lightning flashing from the Hayyot's radiance
was the appearance of the [High] Priest.

The שְׁלִיחַ צִבּוּר:
אֱמֶת, מַה נֶּהְדָּר הָיָה כֹהֵן גָּדוֹל
בְּצֵאתוֹ מִבֵּית קָדְשֵׁי הַקֳּדָשִׁים בְּשָׁלוֹם בְּלִי פֶגַע.

*The following piyut was traditionally recited responsively,
the שְׁלִיחַ צִבּוּר chanting each line and the קָהָל responding with
"מַרְאֵה כֹהֵן." In some congregations, the whole piyut is sung collectively.*

כְּאֹהֶל הַנִּמְתָּח בְּדָרֵי מַעְלָה   מַרְאֵה כֹהֵן
כִּבְרָקִים הַיּוֹצְאִים מִזִּיו הַחַיּוֹת   מַרְאֵה כֹהֵן

Why was the Kohen Gadol so joyous after he finished his service in the Temple? How should that impact on what we feel on Yom Kippur? Do you see Yom Kippur as a burden or a day of opportunity? How does Yom Kippur inspire you with a sense of destiny and mission, especially when looking back at our history?

Choose Life!

Naftali Lau-Lavie

In Balaam's Prophecy, Naftali-Lau-Lavie reflects on his feelings at the moment when his brother and fellow Holocaust survivor, Rabbi Yisrael Meir Lau, was installed as Chief Rabbi of Israel.

Naftali Lau-Lavie

L ooking back on a process begun half a century ago, from our state of utter vulnerability to our state of sovereignty, and looking ahead to assess the daunting obstacles still in our path, I cling to the fervent hope that we will ultimately achieve our national aspirations, our cherished goal of living in peace amongst nations.

Deep in my heart I still sense the stubborn resolve to survive, the injunction to "choose life" that helped us to survive then, amid the cinders, and now, surrounded by enemies who seek our destruction. The experience of our past has forged us and bolstered our collective resolve to pave a road that, I pray, will lead to a new Jewish society, self-reliant and just, with only minimal political, social, and religious tensions. As I survey my own experiences and the way the seemingly impossible became possible, repeatedly emerging from labyrinths that perplexed us, my certainty grows that we will find the strength to achieve our objectives: First and foremost, the guarantee of our continued national existence, and the creation of a healthy and prosperous society that will serve as a light to world Jewry.

> *The experience of our past has forged us and bolstered our collective resolve to pave a road that, I pray, will lead to a new Jewish society, self-reliant and just…*

This optimism is based on personal experiences. For fifty years I carried the responsibility passed on to me by my father before he went to his death in Treblinka. He placed in my care a weak child of five, who looked more like a skinny little three-year-old. For three years I served as father and mother, guardian, protector, and mentor to my young brother, Yisrael Meir, or Lulek as we called him then. I feel it was this mission, the mission to bring this brother to safety from the abyss of despair to the gates of hope – to the

Yisrael Meir Lau (8 years old) in the arms of Elazar Schiff,
Buchenwald survivors at their arrival at Haifa on 15 July 1945

Rabbi Yisrael Meir Lau

Promised Land – and thereby guarantee the continuation of our rabbinic dynasty, that kept me alive and gave me the will to fight for our lives rather than succumb to the fate that befell so many of us.

On the first day of the new month of Adar, February 21, 1993, I stood at afternoon prayer with this younger brother at the Western Wall of the Second Temple in Jerusalem. It was the same spot where we had stood forty-eight years earlier, on our arrival in Jerusalem. Then, as an eight-year-old, he had gazed at the stones of the Western Wall without any appreciation or awareness of its significance. This time he was praying for divine guidance before assuming the highest post of any rabbi in Israel. My young brother, who had come forth from the ashes of the death camps, was shortly to be proclaimed Chief Rabbi of Israel. I looked at him with tears of pride and gratitude - and relief that my mission was at last fulfilled.

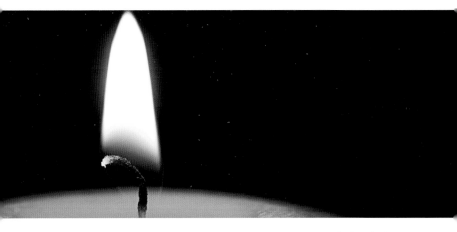

YIZKOR

יזכור

(i) The memorial service recited on Yom Kippur, the last day of Pesach, the second day of Shavuot and Shemini Atzeret.

For one's father:

יִזְכֹּר May God remember the soul of my revered father (*name* son of *father's name*) who has gone to his everlasting home. May his soul be bound in the bond of life. May his rest be with honour, fullness of joy in Your presence, and bliss at Your right hand for evermore. Amen.

For one's mother:

יִזְכֹּר May God remember the soul of my revered mother (*name* daughter of *father's name*) who has gone to her everlasting home. May her soul be bound in the bond of life. May her rest be with honour, fullness of joy in Your presence, and bliss at Your right hand for evermore. Amen.

For one's father:

יִזְכֹּר אֱלֹהִים נִשְׁמַת אָבִי מוֹרִי (פלוני בן פלוני) שֶׁהָלַךְ לְעוֹלָמוֹ, אָנָּא תְּהִי נַפְשׁוֹ צְרוּרָה בִּצְרוֹר הַחַיִּים, וּתְהִי מְנוּחָתוֹ כָּבוֹד, שֹׂבַע שְׂמָחוֹת אֶת־פָּנֶיךָ, נְעִמוֹת בִּימִינְךָ נֶצַח: אָמֵן.

For one's mother:

יִזְכֹּר אֱלֹהִים נִשְׁמַת אִמִּי מוֹרָתִי (פלונית בת פלוני) שֶׁהָלְכָה לְעוֹלָמָהּ, אָנָּא תְּהִי נַפְשָׁהּ צְרוּרָה בִּצְרוֹר הַחַיִּים, וּתְהִי מְנוּחָתָהּ כָּבוֹד, שֹׂבַע שְׂמָחוֹת אֶת־פָּנֶיךָ, נְעִמוֹת בִּימִינְךָ נֶצַח: אָמֵן.

 Why do we recite Yizkor prayers on Yom Kippur? How might God 'remember' people who have passed away? What should we do to remember them? What messages does this give us on Yom Kippur?

Yizkor and Yom Kippur

ne tradition which some families have, in common with many others, is to write the names and yahrzeit (date of passing in the Jewish calendar) details of deceased relatives on a slip of paper at the back of a Yom Kippur machzor (prayer book).

When Yizkor prayers are recited, these details, which sadly but inevitably grow longer with the passing of time, help us to recall, even fleetingly, both close and distant relatives, those who we knew and those who unfortunately we did not meet. Some of the memories are warm, others are raw, whilst for some relatives or martyrs, painfully, there are no memories to recall at all.

The 'ultimate' recollection belongs to God, which makes Yizkor particularly appropriate for Yom Kippur. The Torah refers to Yom Kippur in the plural, Yom Hakippurim, from which the renowned medieval German scholar Marhari Weil (quoted by the halachic work Darchei Moshe, Orach Chaim 621) teaches that atonement therefore applies to both the living and the dead. This may explain why Yizkor was originally said only on Yom Kippur, apparently introduced amongst Ashkenazi Jews as a prayer for and memorial to those Jews murdered during the Crusades.

Sadly, of course, the Crusades are not the only tragedy which our people has faced and the Yizkor prayers have expanded over the years to reflect this. Amongst the most moving moments in recent years at Finchley Synagogue (Kinloss) have been when Rev Simon Hass, one of the greatest chazanim in the world who served the Central Synagogue in Great Portland Street for many years before retiring to Finchley, has led some of the Yizkor prayers on Yom Kippur. The prayers of Rev Hass, who grew up in Eastern Europe and survived several concentration camps, are spine-tingling, especially when praying for those murdered Jews of whom there are no memories anymore.

Why do we use the word Yizkor, which here literally means 'he [God] will remember', especially since God does not forget? We might suggest an answer from the earliest use of this verb in the Torah, chapter 8 of Bereishit (Genesis), which teaches that God remembered (Vayizkor) Noah after the waters of the flood had subsided.

The commentator Rashi (1040-1105) explains that Vayizkor refers to God's attribute of judgment. The prayers of the righteous can turn judgment into mercy. The Torah describes Noah as righteous, from which the commentator Ramban (1190-1274), understands that Noah's righteousness and God's covenant with Noah to save him were what God 'remembered' at that time.

This teaches a powerful lesson about Yizkor prayers. God does not forget and does not need prompting to remember. Yet when we pray sincerely, especially on Yom Kippur, we have the opportunity to establish ourselves as righteous and turn judgment to mercy. We also express our acceptance as descendants of Avraham, Yitzchak and Yaakov of His covenants with them to guarantee the future of the Jewish people, an acceptance which is part of our daily prayers and particularly prevalent in Yom Kippur prayers.

Yizkor therefore is not just our prayer to God for deceased relatives and martyrs. It is also a plea that He should always relate to them in Heaven with mercy, continually extending the atonement to which Mahari Weil referred.

Some years ago, I was fortunate to visit the quaint little shul in Llandudno, North Wales, retracing my wife's family roots in the town. Looking at the memorial boards, I saw mention made of several of her relatives. This made it particularly poignant to say Mincha (the afternoon prayers) in a shul where four generations ago her family had prayed and to reflect on how they had bequeathed Judaism to us. It also enabled me to add their details to the slip of paper in my Yom Kippur machzor and to consider how perhaps our practice of Judaism in some way helps our deceased relatives be granted the remembrance by God that we pray for in Yizkor.

May God answer all of our prayers favourably and always 'remember' for the good, those no longer with us.

Tell our Story – Some Thoughts for Yizkor
Rabbi Lord Sacks

A memorial and tribute evening was held at the Western Marble Arch Synagogue on 24 November 2015 in memory of the outstanding historian, Sir Martin Gilbert, who published almost 80 books. Guests from around the world included rabbis, diplomats, academics, politicians, soldiers, intelligence officers and students of Sir Martin.

They were welcomed by Lady Esther Gilbert before Rabbi Nicky Liss, Sir Martin's rabbi at Highgate Synagogue, introduced The Rt Hon. Gordon Brown, Rabbi Lord Jonathan Sacks, Professor Sir Richard Evans and Randolph Churchill who gave their personal tributes in honour of Sir Martin. Rabbi Lionel Rosenfeld of the Western Marble Arch Synagogue recited the Memorial Prayer.

Rabbi Sacks' moving tribute appears below. It emphasises several themes relating to our Yizkor prayers, especially considering how to remember the impact of those sadly no longer with us. The other eulogies and more about Sir Martin appear at www. sirmartingilbert.com

Distinguished Rabbanim, your Excellencies, Lords, Ladies, Friends. Martin was such a very special person. We loved him, we admired him, we miss him. But I find my mind going back to a moment when it just overwhelmed me what Martin had actually done to earn a place in all our hearts.

It must have been 15 years ago, just before the Holocaust Exhibition was opened in the Imperial War Museum. The organisers of that wonderful exhibition had decided in their thoughtfulness and kindness to invite the Holocaust survivors to a dinner in the Imperial War Museum just a couple of weeks before the exhibition was opened, so that they could see it first.

I was dreading that moment, I thought it would open up the trauma all over again. I didn't know how they were going to face that evening. That night Sir Martin and myself were the speakers. I needn't have worried, they were exuberant. It was as if they were at a wedding. They proceeded to talk non-stop through my speech, through Martin's speech.

I asked them, why are you so cheerful? They said to me you don't realise, until this exhibition was opened, we didn't know who would care for our memories when we are no longer here. But now that the exhibition is there, we feel safe, that burden has been lifted from us. And it was at that moment that I suddenly realised that Martin telling the story of the Holocaust and so many other stories had lifted a burden from so many broken hearts and given people a sense of permanence, a sense of being remembered, and being heard. Martin was the person who gave a voice to the voiceless. And although Martin was, and will be rightly remembered as one of the world's great historians of our time, of Churchill, of the Second World War and of so many other things, I just want to speak this evening of how Martin was a Jewish historian specifically in two ways.

Martin telling the story of the Holocaust and so many other stories had lifted a burden from so many broken hearts and given people a sense of permanence…

Number one, he told the Jewish story as it needed to be told through the eye and the hand of the master. He told the story of the Jews of the former Soviet Union, the Jews, as Elie Wiesel called them, 'of silence', but as Martin called them, 'of hope'. And he gave them hope. He wrote brilliant histories of Israel, of Jerusalem and of course the Holocaust.

One of his loveliest books came about in this peculiar way. Martin had known a very distinguished Indian lady, Lady Nehru, who was the mother of a friend of his from Oxford. For years he kept in touch with her. Then on her 90th birthday she finally confided in Martin that she wasn't an Indian of noble birth, she was actually a Hungarian Jew.

And she said 'I always wanted to know the story of this identity of which I have only just revealed. Could you tell me the story of the Jewish people?' Well the Jewish people have been around a fair time – for over five thousand years. Martin agreed and proceeded, over the next several years, to write the story of the Jewish people in a series of letters and postcards to Auntie Fori as he called her. Those letters were published in one of the most delightful charming ways of telling our story that I have ever come across

and how moved I am that Auntie Fori's son, Aditya Nehru, is with us this evening.

One of the last books he wrote was 'In Ishmael's House, the story of Jews in Muslim lands'. And if I'm not mistaken Martin was engaged before his terrible illness in telling the Jewish story of the contribution to Britain which I hope will be told. And throughout this wondrous work he told the Jewish story.

But the second point I make is that Martin in a deeper sense understood that by being a historian, he was showing us one way in which to serve God himself. He understood something more powerfully than anyone I

… Martin in a deeper sense understood that by being a historian, he was showing us one way in which to serve God himself.

ever met, that history is a profoundly Jewish vocation. It was the American Jewish historian Yosef Chaim Yerushalmi who pointed out that Jews were the first people to see God in history, not just in nature. The first people to see history as a continuing narrative, with a beginning, a middle and a distantly good end. Isaiah Berlin wrote that all Jews who are at all conscious of their identity as Jews, are steeped in history. And in one of the most extraordinary moments that I ever read about, the great Jewish historian, Simon Dubnow, 81 years old, in the Riga Ghetto in December 1941 was shot by the Nazis, and his dying words, according to the story told, were 'Yidn, shraybt un farshraybt', 'Jews, write and record'. Tell our story. And that is what Martin gave to us all.

He understood that to be a Jew, even in the days of the Temple, is to get up every year bringing first fruits and say, 'Arami oved avi', my father was a wondering Aramean, the first ever people to make memory a religious duty.

There was one line in the last speech Moses ever gave in his life that Martin had engraved in his heart and he wrote it and mentions it in his books. Moses tells the future generation, 'Zechor yemot olam' – remember the days of old. 'Bino shenot dor vador' – meditate on the history of previous generations. And that was the religious task Martin did. He turned our history into our memory and thus served God in this most beautiful of ways.

Many years ago when I was Chief Rabbi, my team devised an award system for Anglo Jewry of the people and programmes and institutions of which we were most proud. And we held back one specific award which I was given the privilege of giving personally to the person who, in my opinion, exemplified all that was best in Jewish life and did so while contributing to society as a whole. I had not the slightest hesitation in giving that award to Martin Gilbert. Never have I made a decision that was more agreed with because he was a source of pride to every one of us.

He turned our history into our memory and thus served God in this most beautiful of ways.

Friends, Martin was a great scholar, a great mensch, a great Jew. A man who made friends wherever he went and kept all those friendships. A man of truth who recorded the facts and then let them speak for themselves. And we all feel a sense of loss. Martin loved every member of his extended family and was given so much by every one of them. But I must say, just personally, how unbelievably moving I found the way Esther cared for him in those last difficult years with such sensitivity, and such grace and such fortitude. It was moving beyond words to see. And Esther and all of Martin's extended family, may God send you comfort in the knowledge of this remarkable man that you and we were privileged to know.

The rabbis said 'ain osim nefashot l'zadikim – divreihem ain heim zichronam' – we don't make monuments for those who have died. Their words are their memorial. Martin gave so many people their memorial in words. We will never forget him. Yehi Zichro Baruch and his memory will always be a blessing. Amen.

Photo courtesy of www.45aid.org. Formed in 1963 by a group of Holocaust survivors known as 'The Boys', the '45 Aid Society aims to look after survivors, give back to society and teach the lessons of the Holocaust to future generations. For many years, Sir Martin Gilbert was President and Sir Ben Helfgott was Chairman of the '45 Aid Society. The Society is now run by the second generation, the children and grandchildren of 'The Boys'.

YONA

יוֹנָה

ⓘ The biblical book of Jonah, recited in the afternoon prayers of Yom Kippur.

1 The word of the LORD came to Jonah son of Amittai:
2 Go at once to Nineveh, that great city, and proclaim judgment upon it; for their wickedness has come before Me.
3 Jonah, however, started out to flee to Tarshish from the LORD's service. He went down to Joppa and found a ship going to Tarshish. He paid the fare and went aboard to sail with the others to Tarshish, away from the service of the LORD.

א וַיְהִי דְּבַר־יְהֹוָה אֶל־יוֹנָה בֶן־אֲמִתַּי לֵאמֹר׃
ב קוּם לֵךְ אֶל־נִינְוֵה הָעִיר הַגְּדוֹלָה וּקְרָא עָלֶיהָ
כִּי־עָלְתָה רָעָתָם לְפָנָי׃
ג וַיָּקָם יוֹנָה לִבְרֹחַ תַּרְשִׁישָׁה מִלִּפְנֵי יְהֹוָה וַיֵּרֶד
יָפוֹ וַיִּמְצָא אֳנִיָּה ׀ בָּאָה תַרְשִׁישׁ וַיִּתֵּן שְׂכָרָהּ
וַיֵּרֶד בָּהּ לָבוֹא עִמָּהֶם תַּרְשִׁישָׁה מִלִּפְנֵי יְהֹוָה׃

  In the following article, Pnina Savery considers some of the big questions from Sefer Yona and provides discussion points.

Getting to Grips with
Sefer Yona (the book of Jonah)
Pnina Savery

Yona is one of the most famous biblical stories, and certainly the most well-known of the books of the Trei Asar, the Twelve Minor Prophets. Read as the haftarah at Mincha (afternoon prayers) on Yom Kippur, it tells the story of the prophet who, reluctant to carry out his mission, attempts to run away from God. Yona hides in a boat bound for a distant land. However, he cannot escape his destiny and is swallowed by a fish. Ultimately he is forced to deliver his prophecy to the people of Nineveh, a large Assyrian city far away from the Land of Israel and Jewish life. The result is that they repent successfully and are forgiven for their sins.

Sefer Yona raises many profound questions and this is perhaps one of the reasons that it is read on Yom Kippur…

Sefer Yona raises many profound questions and this is perhaps one of the reasons that it is read on Yom Kippur, a day when our prayers and observances encourage us to consider such questions. We shall raise such questions here, with some suggested discussion points. If you have the chance, read Sefer Yona first in either Hebrew or English (it should take no longer than about 15-20 minutes) but if not, continue below.

1. Why would a prophet of God run away from his Divine task?

Rabbi Avraham Ibn Ezra (c.1089-1164) explains that Yona was not running away from God; rather he was running from a message with which he disagreed. This explanation becomes clearer when we view Yona in context. With his full name of Yona ben Amitai, Yona is also mentioned in Sefer Melachim (2 Kings 14:25). Read the following verses:

מלכים ב פרק יד

בִּשְׁנַת חֲמֵשׁ־עֶשְׂרֵה שָׁנָה לַאֲמַצְיָהוּ בֶן־יוֹאָשׁ מֶלֶךְ יְהוּדָה מָלַךְ יָרָבְעָם
בֶּן־יוֹאָשׁ מֶלֶךְ־יִשְׂרָאֵל בְּשֹׁמְרוֹן אַרְבָּעִים וְאַחַת שָׁנָה: וַיַּעַשׂ הָרַע בְּעֵינֵי
יְקֹוָק לֹא סָר מִכָּל־חַטֹּאות יָרָבְעָם בֶּן־נְבָט אֲשֶׁר הֶחֱטִיא אֶת־יִשְׂרָאֵל:
הוּא הֵשִׁיב אֶת־גְּבוּל יִשְׂרָאֵל מִלְּבוֹא חֲמָת עַד־יָם הָעֲרָבָה כִּדְבַר יְקֹוָק
אֱלֹהֵי יִשְׂרָאֵל אֲשֶׁר דִּבֶּר בְּיַד־עַבְדּוֹ יוֹנָה בֶן־אֲמִתַּי הַנָּבִיא אֲשֶׁר מִגַּת
הַחֵפֶר:

2 Kings Chapter 14
23) In the fifteenth year of King Amaziah son of Yoash of Judah, King Yerovam son of Yoash of Israel became king in Samaria for forty-one years. 24) He did what was displeasing to the Lord; he did not depart from all the sins that Yarovam son of Nevat had caused Israel to commit. 25) It was he who restored the territory of Israel from Levo-chamat to the sea of the Aravah, in accordance with the promise that the Lord, the God of Israel, had made through His servant, the prophet Yona son of Amitai from Gat-chepher.

How is Yerovam ben Yoash, the King of Israel described? How might Yona have felt delivering a prophecy regarding restoring territory to him?

Yona struggled with the concept that a sinful king would be rewarded with expanding the borders of the land. This did not fit with his worldview of strict din (judgement), i.e. that the righteous are rewarded and the sinners are punished. When Yona was sent by God to Nineveh, he rebelled against this idea. He did not think it was right for God's rachamim (mercy) to allow the repentant sinners of Nineveh to be let off again. He did not want to be, yet again, the prophet to reward sinners. Yona wanted to root out all sin from the world. To achieve this, sin needed to be punished.

> *Yona wanted to root out all sin from the world. To achieve this, sin needed to be punished.*

How does this message link to the concepts of Yom Kippur that we recite in our prayers? Do you agree with Yona's approach? Based on your answers, why do you think Sefer Yona is recited during the Mincha prayers on Yom Kippur?

2. What's the significance of the kikayon (bush) at the end?

By the final chapter of the book, Yona is angry with God. He does not understand why God has accepted Nineveh's repentance, so God uses a kikayon to teach him a lesson. Yona is suffering in the hot sun and God provides him with the shade of the bush to alleviate this. This causes Yona "great happiness" (4:6). Just as quickly, God sends a worm to destroy the bush, leaving Yona to agonise in the heat of the day and asking to die instead of suffer (4:7-8). The kikayon represents God's rachamim: his merciful lessening of Yona's discomfort, even if Yona has done nothing to deserve it.

The removal of the kikayon represents a life of strict din. God shows Yona what a world without God's mercy is like, the way that Yona apparently wishes the world would be run. Yet Yona asks to die, even when living in the world that he himself advocates! The lesson is clear: the world cannot run on din alone, rather God's rachamim is essential.

Sefer Yona also captured the interest of secular thinkers. The early Zionist thinker, Asher Zvi Hirsch Ginsberg, (1856-1927, known by his literary name of Achad Ha'am) writes in his 1891 essay "Justice and Mercy" that "Justice seeks to exterminate sin; mercy regards only the sinner".

We can suggest that Yona focused on the sins. He did not give regard to the sinners, the people who had sinned and the circumstances that might have caused them to do so.

How could this relate to our society and justice system today? Consider someone who commits a crime: should the judgment instigate punishment based only on the sin, or should it take into account the situation of the sinner too?

3. What is the overall significance of the book of Yona?
Read the following commentary of the Radak (acronym for Rabbi David Kimchi, 1160–1235) to the first verse of Sefer Yona – "And the word of God came to Yona ben Amitai, saying…" - and consider the three answers the Radak offers.

> *Radak on Yona 1:1 - We could ask, why was this prophecy of Yona included in our Tanach (Hebrew Bible), when the whole story is concerning other nations of the world with no mention of the Jewish people at all? Sefer Yona is the only book in Tanach in which Jews play no role.*
>
> *(1) It is possible to explain that Sefer Yona was written as reprimand to the Jewish people: that a non-Jewish nation repented the first time they heard rebuke from a prophet, whilst the Jewish nation did not listen to the prophets who reproached them in the name of God day and night [for the sins they committed and the effects these caused].*
>
> *(2) Another answer is that Sefer Yona describes the great miracles that God did for the prophet [Yona], for example, by keeping him alive in the fish for three days and three nights.*
>
> *(3) Additionally, the story tells us that God has mercy on all of His creatures, and certainly for those who repent.*

Which of these three reasons do you consider the most important? Based on what we have discussed so far, are you able to suggest any other reasons why Yona is included in our Tanach?

A contemporary message for Sefer Yona

One of the fundamental messages of Yona is the openness and availability of teshuva (repentance). It is never too late for us to repent for our sins and to reconnect to God. Although we never hear a response from Yona, the Midrashic collection in the Yalkut Shimoni (rabbinic teachings sourced from the Tanach) shows that he realises by the end of the book that it is impossible to run the world according to din alone. Instead, we require God's rachamim as well.

On Yom Kippur, we entreat God to regard only the sinner, instead of the sin. We pray to God repeatedly to run the world with rachamim, not just din. We call out to God, 'reminding' Him that even the most righteous individual cannot refrain from sin altogether, thereby requiring both rachamim, not din alone. We pray that God will accept our teshuva and inscribe us in the Book of Life, just as the people of Nineveh and Yona were allowed to live, despite having previously broken God's word.

"To go to Jerusalem, it is enough to have the clothes you stand up in."

NEILA

נעילה

(i) The closing service unique to Yom Kippur.

Our Father, our King, bring us back to You in perfect repentance.

Our Father, our King, send a complete healing to the sick of Your people.

Our Father, our King, tear up the evil decree against us.

Our Father, our King, remember us with a memory of favourable deeds before You.

Our Father, our King, seal us in the book of good life.

Our Father, our King, seal us in the book of redemption and salvation.

Our Father, our King, seal us in the book of livelihood and sustenance.

Our Father, our King, seal us in the book of merit.

Our Father, our King, seal us in the book of pardon and forgiveness.

אָבִינוּ מַלְכֵּנוּ, הַחֲזִירֵנוּ בִּתְשׁוּבָה שְׁלֵמָה לְפָנֶיךָ.

אָבִינוּ מַלְכֵּנוּ, שְׁלַח רְפוּאָה שְׁלֵמָה לְחוֹלֵי עַמֶּךָ.

אָבִינוּ מַלְכֵּנוּ, קְרַע רֹעַ גְּזַר דִּינֵנוּ.

אָבִינוּ מַלְכֵּנוּ, זָכְרֵנוּ בְּזִכָּרוֹן טוֹב לְפָנֶיךָ.

אָבִינוּ מַלְכֵּנוּ, חָתְמֵנוּ בְּסֵפֶר חַיִּים טוֹבִים.

אָבִינוּ מַלְכֵּנוּ, חָתְמֵנוּ בְּסֵפֶר גְּאֻלָּה וִישׁוּעָה.

אָבִינוּ מַלְכֵּנוּ, חָתְמֵנוּ בְּסֵפֶר פַּרְנָסָה וְכַלְכָּלָה.

אָבִינוּ מַלְכֵּנוּ, חָתְמֵנוּ בְּסֵפֶר זְכֻיּוֹת.

אָבִינוּ מַלְכֵּנוּ, חָתְמֵנוּ בְּסֵפֶר סְלִיחָה וּמְחִילָה.

The Leader recites each of the following three verses, followed by the congregation, aloud and in unison:

Listen, Israel: the LORD is our God, the LORD is One.

The שליח ציבור recites each of the following three verses, followed by the קהל, aloud and in unison:

שְׁמַע יִשְׂרָאֵל, יְהוה אֱלֹהֵינוּ, יְהוה אֶחָד:

The Leader three times, then the congregation three times:

Blessed be the name of His glorious kingdom for ever and all time.

The שליח ציבור three times, then the קהל three times:

בָּרוּךְ שֵׁם כְּבוֹד מַלְכוּתוֹ לְעוֹלָם וָעֶד.

The Leader seven times, then the congregation seven times:

The LORD He is God.

The שליח ציבור seven times, then the קהל seven times:

יהוה הוּא הָאֱלֹהִים.

Congregation aloud:

Next year in Jerusalem rebuilt!

Congregation aloud:

לְשָׁנָה הַבָּאָה בִּירוּשָׁלַיִם הַבְּנוּיָה.

Why do we end Neila with these dramatic declarations? What takeaway messages do they give you from Yom Kippur? How have they sustained Jews throughout the ages?

The Crescendo that is Neila

Rabbi Major Reuven Livingstone

Neila, or "the closing of the gates," is the very final chance on Yom Kippur to ask God for forgiveness; as the well-known piyut (poem) says, "Find for us forgiveness at this hour of the closing of the gates." Apart from being the culmination of our Yamim Noraim prayers and, unusually, a fourth daytime service, Neila is unique among all other prayers of the year. On all other days we have separate services, but on Yom Kippur, we have an almost continuous 'day of prayer', with Neila serving as the culmination or crescendo. It is as if a person who has not prayed the others has lost the opportunity to pray Neila. It is not free-standing; it cannot fulfil its role on its own.

The last moments of Yom Kippur are often very challenging. We are tired and hungry. The ancient liturgy is often obscure and we do not always understand the words we say... even if we think we do. But there is also an urgent 'now or never' quality to this time. We must pray for our lives, the lives of our families, of our entire nation – and of the wider world too. We must beg and plead as if our existence were at stake, for we believe that this is truly the case.

At the end of Neila (or after the Maariv evening prayers in some communities), we blow the shofar. One reason is that the trumpet is blown to announce that the Shechinah (the Divine Presence) is ascending from the Camp of Israel back to Heaven. Another is to celebrate the triumph and joy of a successful passing of the Day of Forgiveness. According to Rabbi Menachem Mendel of Kotzk (1787-1859), after the shofar was blown following the revelation of the Torah at Sinai, God told Moses to send the Jewish People back to their tents. The true test would begin now. It was relatively easy to stand to attention and submit to the Divine Presence at Mount Sinai. But what would happen when they got back to mundane life? This is a direct parallel to Yom Kippur, the anniversary of the giving of the second set of Tablets. It is easy to make promises and be holy on the holiest day of the year. But the shofar reminds us that God wants to see what we will do when we get home.

But when Neila begins, we are not yet ready for those final shofar blasts. Neila is our final chance to confront our imperfections honestly and take upon ourselves tangible commitments (the original New Year's resolutions!) in order to correct these issues. If we mean it, if we believe in our hearts and minds that we will do better, our prayers will make it past those gates before they lock shut. As another piyut says, "May you merit long years…with joy and gladness (through your teshuva) at the time of the locking of the gates."

We do not have to be instantly perfect - but Neila, as the climax of Yom Kippur and the entire Yamim Noraim, demands concrete steps and honest commitment and the most sincere, heartfelt prayers of the year. It is the time to pray like our lives are truly on the line; for in reality, they are.

Red Sea Spies

THE TRUE STORY
OF MOSSAD'S FAKE
DIVING RESORT

In the mid-1980s, Mossad, Israel's intelligence service, set up a diving resort in Sudan. This provided cover for one of the most remarkable missions ever undertaken by the State of Israel, the clandestine operation to move thousands of Ethiopian Jews to Israel, via Sudan.

This was not an operation with simply a Zionist objective. Ethiopia and Sudan were dangerous places to be Jews yet had a remarkable Jewish community, largely cut off from the rest of the world, but have much to teach about what commitment to Judaism and Israel means as we recite the concluding words of the Neila prayers.

We pick up their story with Avrehet, a grandmother, whose nephew, Ferede Aklum, had managed to escape to Israel. Ferede had helped other Jews to escape. He had managed to send a message home indicating that it was now possible, despite a dangerous, arduous journey, to leave the village where she has always lived and travel to Israel.

The Jews who trekked from their villages in the Ethiopian Highlands to Sudan left behind not only the places where their ancestors had dwelt for centuries, but also their way of life. No one knew just how perilous the journey would be. Some thought it would take only hours. For many it took months. The way was merciless.

Yet, despite this, they would not be deterred from their objective: to reach Jerusalem.

The following are abridged extracts from chapter five of 'Red Sea Spies: The True Story of the Mossad's Fake Diving Resort', by Raffi Berg, which inspired Netflix's 'The Red Sea Diving Resort'.

The family got together to decide what to do. The atmosphere was different. Avrehet declared she would leave immediately. Some chose to go with her. Others said they would follow on later.

Avrehet had already gathered information from traders about the route and what was in store. She assembled a group of fourteen people, comprising one of her daughters, her daughter's family and two families of friends. The group included young children, one of whom was just three months old. Avrehet's two other daughters stayed behind. Yazezow

> '*To go to Jerusalem,' Avrehet said, 'it is enough to have the clothes you stand up in.'*

said he would also go after he had organised the sale of his house and land. Avrehet's group left at night, so as not to alert any non-Jewish villagers to their departure. They left behind almost everything they owned.

'To go to Jerusalem,' Avrehet said, 'it is enough to have the clothes you stand up in.'

Word started to spread, from Jew to Jew and village to village, that some of the community had secretly left for the Land of Jerusalem. One of those who heard about it was Zehava Gedamo, then a young girl.

'People started to tell us that many people were walking to Jerusalem. This was a distant dream for us. Someone dreams all day, and when the dream comes true he doesn't believe it, and then he starts to dream again. [I] took [my] mother's hand and thought to [myself]: "We're going to Jerusalem. Everyone is going there, and now we are too. We are going to Jerusalem, which is all golden, even the earth and the stones, and there is always a rainbow and a golden halo above its sky. It doesn't matter that we're leaving our homes -we're going to a better place, in fact -to the best place in the world."

Indeed, there was a widespread assumption among them that it was not to Sudan that they were walking, but to the Holy City itself.

After centuries of longing, it was felt that the hour of redemption had finally come.

In 1979, just 32 had made it out, while by the end of 1980 the number had soared to about 800, all smuggled through Khartoum Airport.

Benny Ghoshen was five and a half years old when he was collected from his bed by his parents late one night at their home in Adi Woreva. They had chosen Saturday night as departure time, as the Sabbath, when there was no contact between Jewish and Christian neighbours, had just concluded. They crept out of the village in a group of thirteen – the smallest children and elderly people carried on donkeys – and made their way down a valley to the Tekeze River. They went hastily, covering the 25 kilometres to the river in a day and a half. Benny's parents had had to make the agonising decision that for the sake of their youngest children they would have to go without two of their older sons – one aged sixteen, who had been forced into the TPLF (an Ethiopian rebel movement), and another aged eighteen, who was working elsewhere as a teacher.

At the river they converged with Jews who had come from other villages as part of a plan to go en masse, until there were about 400 people walking together. They crossed the river, wading through on foot, or by horse or donkey. Some of the youngest children fell off into the water and had to be saved from drowning, but everyone eventually made it to the other side. After days and nights of more journeying – moving only after dark so as not to be seen – the group arrived at the Wolkait mountain range. With the rugged escarpments rising thousands of feet above them, the tired throng began its long and difficult ascent.

The crossing took days, stopping when it was light and carrying on at night. The terrain transformed, from lush and verdant to arid and barren, where it became a matter of survival. Provisions of water were running so low that they started to ration portions to three bottle caps a day for children, and just one for adults. What little food they had left was also divided into morsels.

Weaker people in the group fell ill, and some died. Benny, who had been walking barefoot on scorching sand, was suffering from exhaustion, so was put on the back of a donkey. As they continued, the animals suddenly went wild and started to stampede. They had seen a small pool of water and, dying of thirst, charged towards it. As Benny's donkey ran, he was struck by the branch of a tree and fell off. He lay where he landed, showing no signs of life. Members of the group checked him but were convinced he was dead, another tragic casualty of the brutal trek. They decided to bury him and dug a grave, but the Jewish custom of ritual purity was so strictly observed by the Beta Israel that even in the desert they would not put a body in the ground unclean.

With water from the pool, they started to wash him, whereupon Benny began to move. To the shock of everyone, the boy started crying. He had been knocked unconscious but the water brought him round.

Three months after leaving their village, they finally arrived at the camp. Within days, Benny's family were smuggled out and driven to Khartoum. Ferede got them passports and they were put on a flight to Marseille.

There they switched to an El Al plane, and on 25 May 1980 they landed in Israel. As a child, Benny did not know what an aeroplane was, and would playfully throw stones at the sky whenever one flew overhead. By the age of 30, he was a major in the Israeli Air Force…

… At the close of Yom Kippur when we proclaim 'next year in Jerusalem', we wish you well for the year ahead. We hope that you will take inspiration for the year ahead from the incredible people you have just read about, so that you too will be blessed to continue creating the ongoing story of the Jewish people, rooted in our faith, beliefs, mitzvot and traditions.

Chag Sameach for Succot and see you in Jerusalem!

The Holy Pub

I would like to share one of my favourite Jewish stories with you, one which I think of each year as Rosh Hashana, Yom Kippur and Succot draw close. I hope you too will find it as impactful I do.

The scene is in Berdichev, now in Ukraine, but previously in Czarist Russia, some time in the late 18th century. The rabbi of the town, known after it as Rabbi Levi Yitzchak of Berdichev, was one of the leading figures of the nascent Chasidic movement. Such was his impact on the town, especially demonstrated through his love, compassion and care for others, not just his scholarship, that after his passing in 1809, the community never officially appointed a rabbi in his place.

Here follows a version of the story in brief. It can be found in greater detail in *Loving & Beloved, Tales of Rabbi Levi Yitzchak of Berdichev, Defender of Israel* by Simcha Raz, translated by Dov Peretz Elkins, Menorah Books 2016.

... In one of the many Jewish villages throughout Poland and Ukraine, there was an inn near a main road frequented by travelling merchants. The innkeeper was a Jew named Mendel, known simply as Mendel the Innkeeper. In particular, Mendel was renowned for the warmth of his welcome. If there was a knock on the door, even late on a chilly winter night, Mendel would rise and open up. A warm bed and meal awaited the weary traveller, even if the traveller had to put the cost on his tab.

As Mendel grew old, he became restless. Finally, he summoned Sheike, his son. "For so much of my life, I have had to serve drinks and run a pub. I barely have time to pray and I hardly know our prayers anyway. Even when I can pray in shul on Yom Kippur, I cannot really follow.

"I must prepare for the future.

"Sheike, my son, you will now manage the inn. I shall retire to the city.

"At last, I will learn to daven and understand the chumash."

As Mendel went to the city, Sheike took over. The inn was no longer Mendel's.

Exhausted travellers, whether they arrived early or late, did not receive the warm welcome to which they had become accustomed.

Word soon got out to the Jewish pedlars. Avoid this inn. Yet where else would they go?

Before long, this news reached Rabbi Levi Yitzchak. Immediately, he asked to speak to Mendel. "Why did you retire?" asked the rabbi.

Pouring out his heart, Mendel explained. "I am fearful of appearing before the Heavenly Court with no mitzvot in hand. At last, I can grasp this opportunity, to daven, to learn, to acquire mitzvot."

Rabbi Levi Yitzchak stayed silent, deep in thought. Finally, he smiled at Mendel. "My dear friend. You know, the Holy One, blessed be He, gives each Jew their own mission in the world, their own place. Each Jew must fulfil that mission and not the mission of somebody else.

"A private who leaves his post in the army and acts like a general is as if a deserter. The Jewish people have many with the privilege of great learning, akin to our generals. It needs the ordinary Jews, living Jewish lives with devotion every day. God gives one person their mission in the Beit Midrash (study hall), the other at an inn.

"Mendel, my dear friend. You know what has happened to your inn. You also know what needs to happen there.

"Go back, please, with the learning and davening you have achieved in hand. Develop it as much as you can. But remember, perhaps God has given you the mission of looking after weary travellers.

"And as much as I can guarantee, you will after 120 years stand in heaven as a man wealthy in mitzvot. Every meal you have served, every warm bed you have prepared, will stand beside you.

"Go please, Mendel, return to your inn. And may God bless you in all that you do." Mendel looked intently at the rabbi, and returned to the inn.

This story challenges me, especially as I prepare for the holy days ahead. There are several characters in the story: Mendel – both the Mendel who wishes to retire and Mendel the innkeeper; Sheike; the rabbi; the travellers and of course God.

Which character am I at the moment? Which character should I be? How do I relate to the other characters? What is my mission? These are important questions for me, particularly at this time of the year. This story helps me to reflect on them and I hope it will help you as well.

May God answer our prayers favourably, to grant us and the whole world a year ahead full of blessing.

The Ultimate Prayer Recipe

Rabbi Eli Levin

How meaningful is prayer to you? Watch this short video that Tribe made at JFS (https://tinyurl.com/y3reck3y) and enjoy a debate with family & friends, perhaps around your dinner table. Here are some ideas to include in your discussion...

You are sitting in shul or at home on Yom Kippur, counting down the hours of the fast and how many pages are left in the machzor. There is still a long way to go. A lot has happened in your life since last Yom Kippur and in a way this would be a great time to reflect on it all. You think to yourself, isn't that what prayer is – connecting with God about my own life? Yet the marathon of Yom Kippur prayers might seem far from this. The authors knew nothing about my life. I might know little of their words and their meaning. If this is what prayer has become, are we missing the point?

To answer this question, let us look at some amazing examples of prayers from Jewish history, which provide the basis for our prayers today.

Moses prayed for his sister Miriam to recover from a disease akin to leprosy. He said, "Please God heal her!" (Bemidbar 12:13) His prayer did not need to be any longer because it captured how he felt and his desperate desire for her to recover.

Three centuries later in approximately 931 BCE, Hannah is another individual who underscores the power of prayer. She was distraught that she was childless and went to the Temple to pour out her heart before God. Hannah did exactly what she felt and begged God for a child. She did not think about fitting into any mould or having to say any particular words. In fact, she was so lost in her own prayer that Eli, the High Priest, thought she was drunk as she was moving her lips but not making a sound.

Remarkably, when the Talmudic Sages discussed how Jews should pray, they wanted to capture Hannah's passion and so when we pray the quiet Amidah, we move our mouths without making a sound.

These prayers of Moses, Hannah and others, were not found in any siddur or machzor. They were true worship of the heart. Yet, our fixed prayer service looks very different to this. Why?

The story of Hannah, related at the start of the Book of Samuel, was selected as the Haftarah reading for the first day of Rosh Hashanah. This is primarily because one of the themes of Rosh Hashanah and the Yamim Noraim period is zikaron, remembrance. God recalls our actions and we remember Him as our King. Hannah is a prime example of this unique relationship; her story highlights the idea of remembrance. Reading the story of Hannah on the first day of the New Year sets the tone for what prayer means, both at this time of heightened feeling in our lives and also for the months ahead.

Rabbi Adin Steinsaltz (1937-2020), a great contemporary Jerusalem scholar who passed away whilst this article was being written, compares Jewish prayer to a musical performance. The sheet music in front of the musician tells them what music to play, the sequence of notes and the general mood of the piece. However, every artist's rendition will be different. In the end, the performance expresses the musician as much as the composer.

Our sheet music is the prayer book and the people we pray together with are the other members of the orchestra. We are the artists who need to put ourselves into the performance.

There are days when artists feel creative and they just want to play freestyle. There are other times when pouring their heart and soul into Beethoven's symphony is their best form of self-expression. Prayer is exactly like that. There are times when it flows and we just talk to God in our own way using our own language. Yet there is also something about singing off the same sheet that has been used from one generation to the next, connecting ourselves to our heritage while adding our own thoughts, feelings and life experience to the words. Our prayer book is a foundation, not a limitation.

The words of prayer may be ancient, but our feelings can be new every day.

One Akeda Three Stories

Rabbi Cobi Ebrahimoff

The Akeda, the binding of Isaac (Yitzchak) by Abraham (Avraham) as recorded in Bereishit/Genesis ch.22, is the major part of the Torah reading on the second day of Rosh Hashana.

God commands Avraham in his old age to prepare to kill his beloved son Yitzchak, as a sacrifice to God. This is understood with hindsight to be a tenth 'test' for Avraham. He proceeds with perfect faith, until God sends an angel who tells Avraham to stop, signifying that Avraham has passed the test. This passage raises many questions that Jews have studied and discussed through the ages.

In this article, Rabbi Cobi Ebrahimoff, Tribe's Programmes Rabbi, provides some background and analysis of these questions, to help you through the prism of three stories, whether reading by yourself or together with others, to become the next part of that discussion and study through the ages. We hope doing so will enhance your appreciation of this special time of the year and your aspirations for the year ahead.

If you can, read the short passage of the Akeda in your machzor, or in a chumash, and then continue below.

Background to the Akeda and Rosh Hashana

"Blow for Me a ram's shofar, and I shall then remember the binding of Yitzchak" (Talmud, Rosh Hashana 16a).

Akedat Yitzchak (the binding of Yitzchak) represents Avraham's ultimate faith and loyalty. The rabbinic teachings in the work Pesikta Rabbati mention that the story of the Akeda took place on Rosh Hashana. According to some rabbinic sources, Avraham was 137 years old, which means that the Akeda took place on Rosh Hashana 2085 years from the creation of the world.

Avraham is praised unequivocally for his actions as we read on the second day of Rosh Hashana: "Because you have done this and have not withheld your son, your favoured one, I will bestow My blessing upon you and make your descendants as numerous as the stars of heaven and the sand on the seashore" (Bereshit 22:16-17).

We would expect the relationship between Avraham and God to reach new heights following the Akeda. However, in the most crucial moments of the Akeda, God does not appear to Avraham. It was an angel who called out from heaven, instructing Avraham not to slaughter his son. Surprisingly, there is no evidence in the Torah of God speaking to Avraham ever again whilst, paradoxically, before the Akeda, Avraham appears to be in constant conversation with God. For example, Avraham negotiates passionately for the unworthy people of Sodom and even asks God to excuse him while welcoming guests. His conversations with God appear to be frequent and ongoing.

Why does God no longer speak to Avraham?
What happened to Avraham's relationship with God following the Akeda?

We will explore these questions in three ways, telling three distinctively different Akeda stories.

The three approaches in the three stories will focus on Avraham's past, present and future. After learning these three units, you may be able to answer the question in three different ways. You might strongly resonate with some and disagree with others but I hope you will have had fruitful study and discussion nonetheless. That is the beauty of Torah learning!

Story 1:
The Akeda – fixing the past

Avraham was well aware of the sin of Adam and Eve (the name given to the first woman after the sin), which initially expelled us from living an ideal spiritual life in Gan Eden (The Garden of Eden), as recorded in chapter 3 of Bereishit.

Adam and Eve were forced to leave Gan Eden on the day they were created. According to Rabbi Eliezer (Talmud, Rosh Hashana 10b), Adam and Eve were created on the date of Rosh Hashana, which means that they also sinned on Rosh Hashana.

Avraham wanted to renew our bond and connection with God by fixing the sins of the past. Rosh Hashana is therefore the ideal time for Avraham to fix the sins of the past and elevate the world back to the madrega (spiritual level) of Gan Eden.

Adam and Eve were forbidden to eat from Etz HaDa'at (the tree of knowledge). God warns them not to eat from the tree, but the temptation is apparent in the Serpent's words to Eve:

"כִּי בְּיוֹם אֲכָלְכֶם מִמֶּנּוּ וְנִפְקְחוּ עֵינֵיכֶם וִהְיִיתֶם כֵּאלֹהִים יֹדְעֵי טוֹב וָרָע"

"For as soon as you eat from it your eyes will be opened and you will be like God, knowing good and bad."

Adam and Eve understood the importance of following God's command, but they also understood that the Tree Of Knowledge would provide them with independence. The Serpent entices Eve by claiming that they will 'be like God'. Instead of them being recipients of God's command, they will be in command. Avraham wants to atone for their sin by passionately following God's command for the Akeda on the day of Rosh Hashana.

Before the Akeda Avraham prays to save the wicked people of Sedom. Why does he not pray to save his own son?

To continue exploring this approach, we will look at various textual connections in the Torah between Gan Eden and the Akeda, with a particular focus on three 'key' words which are highlighted below.

Hineni!

The episode in Gan Eden ends with Adam and Eve hiding from God among the garden's trees. God calls out to Adam and asks, "Ayekah?" Where are you? God is obviously not inquiring about Adam's physical location; instead, he asks Adam to reconsider his actions. By doing so, God provides Adam with an opportunity to express remorse and repent for his sin. When, though, does an answer to this 'bigger' question of Ayekah appear?

Remarkably, the story of the Akeda begins 2085 years later with Avraham answering clearly as he agrees to follows God's command, **"Hineni!", Here I am!**

HaMakom (the place)

Avraham is sent to Har HaMoriah, Mount Moriah, the very place where we understand that the story of Gan Eden ended. Rabbinic teaching in the Midrash (Pirkei Derabi Eliezer) tell us that Adam and Eve were evicted from Gan Eden and placed on Har HaMoriah. This is the same mountain upon which King Solomon will build the Beit Hamikdash (Temple) some 1000 years after the Akeda. However, you will note in the passage of the Akeda that Avraham is not sent to a mountain called Moriah; rather, he is sent to Eretz HaMoriah (the Land of Moriah). The Midrash (Tanchuma) teaches us that the land was elevated spiritually following the Akeda. The Torah therefore refers to this location as HaMakom, a designated place of holiness.

The Ma'apilim

Intriguingly, the combination of the first two keywords (Hineni and HaMakom) appears elsewhere in the Torah. In the second year after the exodus from Egypt, after the sin of the Meraglim (the spies) who spoke badly about the Land of Israel, Bnei Yisrael (the Israelites) were punished and made to travel in the desert for forty years in total before they could enter the Land. A group of Israelites, who could not tolerate this painful punishment, decide to take immediate action, with the objective of fixing the sin of the Meraglim.

"הִנֶּנּוּ וְעָלִינוּ אֶל הַמָּקוֹם אֲשֶׁר אָמַר ה' כִּי חָטָאנוּ"

"We are ready! We shall ascend to the place of which God has spoken, for we have sinned." *(Bemidbar/Numbers, 14:40)*

This time, the word Hineni appears in the plural as Hinenu. Some of the Israelites were ready and prepared to ascend to HaMakom, the place which God has chosen. Moses warned them that even with all their good intentions, they must not defy God's command. They ignored Moshe's warning and enemies subsequently struck them before reaching the Land of Israel. Those Israelites who attempted to reach HaMakom without seeking God's approval are called Ma'apilim.

In modern Hebrew, the word Ma'apilim is used to describe those Jews who, after World War Two, defiantly travelled to Eretz Yisrael despite the British Mandatory prohibitions on Aliyah (immigration to Israel). Many of the Ma'apilim were Holocaust survivors hoping to start a new life in Israel. Some Ma'apilim were sent back to Europe, but this did not prevent them from trying time and time again. A commemorative coin was issued by the Israeli government in 2007 in honour of the Ma'apilim.

 Look at the unique design on this coin. How does it remind us of the Ma'apilim?

Splitting Wood

Avraham resided in Be'er Sheva, which is in the Negev (southern Israel). Even though there are plenty of trees in the mountains of Jerusalem, close to Eretz HaMoriah, Avraham chopped wood for the offering before embarking on his journey. Surely it would have been more convenient for Avraham to acquire wood in Eretz HaMoriah rather than carrying it from the Negev?

The term Tikkun means 'to fix.' The original sin of Adam and Eve involved a tree, and therefore, Avraham is keen to carry the burden of the tree for the purpose of the Akeda, to perform some sense of Tikkun by use of a tree. Avraham certainly achieves his goal as the Midrash (Mechiltah) teaches us: "In the merit of Avraham splitting the wood, his descendants saw the splitting of the sea," which refers to the miraculous splitting of the sea after the exodus from Egypt.

 What does Tikkun (or the broader phrase, Tikkun Olam, fixing the world) mean in practice and how does it relate to our story?

For those of you who enjoy Gematria (numerical values of Hebrew words), consider the following. The words of this verse: "ויבקע עצי עולה ויקם וילך אל המקום" = He split the wood and went to the designated place", part of the Akeda passage, have the same numerical value as the word בראשית = Bereshit = 907!

The Altar

Avraham arrives in Eretz HaMoriah and builds a Mizbe'ach (altar). The Talmud (Chulin 60a) teaches us that he did not create a new altar; instead, he rebuilt an existing altar.

When Adam and Eve were expelled, we are taught that they offered an offering to God in the same place where the Akeda would later take place, in an attempt to atone for their sins and return to Gan Eden.

This attempt failed because they had not truly repented for the sin; rather, they had only repented for being expelled from Gan Eden. We find a reference to this in the Book of Psalms (69:32):

"וְתִיטַב לַה' מִשּׁוֹר פָּר מַקְרִן מַפְרִיס"

"That will please God more than oxen, than a bull with a horn and hooves."

The verse comes to teach us that true repentance is in the heart and mind, as well as through improving our actions. The offering is only a vehicle for achieving this. Adam and Eve sacrificed their offering without the necessary kavana (sincerity of intention). Avraham did not sacrifice his son, but he was still rewarded for his genuine kavana. Furthermore, the shofar is also called a keren (horn), providing another link to the verse above.

 Nowadays, we are unable to bring korbanot (offerings) since we have no Temple. Can we do teshuva (atone for sins) without korbanot? How?

The Ramban (Rabbi Moshe ben Nachman, 1190-1274) quotes the Midrash (Pirkei D'Rabbi Eliezer) and concludes that the definite article used in the word haMizbe'ach, the altar, to describe the altar that Avraham rebuilt teaches that it was the same altar used by Adam and Eve for their sacrifice:

Once again, Avraham is completing the process of Tikkun by rebuilding the same altar (HaMizbe'ach) in the very same place (HaMakom).

The Angel and the Ram

Avraham's response to the angel teaches us that the Tikkun has not been completed. When the angel commands Avraham not to harm his son, we would

expect Avraham to breathe a sigh of relief and return home. Nevertheless, Avraham is determined to use the altar for something else:

"וַיִּשָּׂא אַבְרָהָם אֶת עֵינָיו וַיַּרְא וְהִנֵּה אַיִל אַחַר נֶאֱחַז בַּסְּבַךְ בְּקַרְנָיו"

"When Avraham looked up, he saw a ram afterwards (achar), caught in the thicket by its horns." (Bereishit 22:13)

Two obvious questions arise from this verse: (1) The word achar seems superfluous in this sentence. (2) What is relevance of the ram being caught in the thicket?

The word achar comes to teach us that this particular ram was prepared, ready, and waiting for this event. The great scholar Rashi (Rabbi Shlomo ben Yitzchak, 1040-1105) explains that the ram had miraculously been waiting "since the six days of creation" to fulfill its duty. The word achar therefore resembles a prolonged and much-anticipated wait.

The 'achar' ram takes us back to the six days of creation or, more specifically, to the sixth day of creation - the day when Adam and Eve sinned.

What, then, is the relevance of the thicket? The Jerusalem Talmud (Ta'anit 2:4) explains the importance of this detail. Until the Akeda, humanity was 'caught' in the sins of the past. For example, the Tree Of Knowledge, the Flood and the Tower of Babylon all represent a downward spiral. Avraham is determined to release us from the thicket of sin and provide us with the opportunity to start afresh on Rosh Hashana

Did the ram enter Noah's ark? If not, how did he survive the flood?

The Site of Sight

The Akeda ends with Avraham naming the mountain upon which the Akeda took place.

"וַיִּקְרָא אַבְרָהָם שֵׁם הַמָּקוֹם הַהוּא ה' יִרְאֶה אֲשֶׁר יֵאָמֵר הַיּוֹם בְּהַר ה' יֵרָאֶה"

"And Avraham named that site Hashem Yireh, as it is said this day, on God's mountain He will be seen"

Avraham completes his Tikkun by giving an additional name to the mountain, as the place where God will be seen. After Adam and Eve ate from the tree of knowledge, "their eyes were opened". They saw the world from a different perspective as they furthered themselves away from their Creator. God calls out to them, asking, "Ayekah?" Desperately asking if they can still see His existence.

The words "Behar Hashem" (on God's mountain) appears three times in the Tanach (Hebrew Bible). What does this resemble?

Avraham completes his Tikkun. On this mountain the Temple (Mikdash) will be built and God will be seen by generations of Jews on Har HaMoriah in Jerusalem.

Story 2:
The Akeda – elevating the present

"וְהָאֱלֹהִים נִסָּה אֶת אַבְרָהָם"
"God tested (nisa) Avraham"

The Nes of Israel

Nisa is a verb. A similar word is nes, which as well as meaning a miracle, also connotes a raised flag, a symbol of triumph and victory. For example, the Biblical prophet Yeshayahu (Isaiah) talks about the times of redemption when the entire world will see the nes of the Jewish people returning to their land:

"כָּל יֹשְׁבֵי תֵבֵל וְשֹׁכְנֵי אָרֶץ כִּנְשֹׂא נֵס הָרִים תִּרְאוּ וְכִתְקֹעַ שׁוֹפָר תִּשְׁמָעוּ"
"All who live in the world And inhabit the earth, When a flag is raised in the hills, take note! When a ram's horn is blown, give heed!" (Isaiah 18:3)

On the 29th November 1947, representatives of many countries gathered in the United Nations Assembly Hall for a crucial debate. The British Mandate was coming to an end, and the proposed partition plan would enable the establishment of a Jewish state and an Arab state in the Land of Israel. A two-thirds majority was necessary to approve the plan. Thirty-three countries (72% of the total vote) voted in favour. Jews worldwide celebrated and raised what would become Israeli flags with pride.

? What did the United Kingdom vote for? Why?

On the 7th June 1967, shortly after the paratroopers entered the Temple Mount and the Kotel area during the Six-Day War, IDF Chief Rabbi Shlomo Goren, arrived holding a Sefer Torah. Rabbi Goren also blew the Shofar as the Israeli soldiers wept tears of joy.

It appeared that the prophecies of Isaiah were fulfilled as a nes, an elevating miracle, in our times.

The Midrash (Raba) mentions that God effectively 'carried' Avraham and uplifted him following the Akeda. The nes of the Akeda sends a strong message to the world: Avraham and his nation are elevated. As we read the story of the Akeda and blow the Shofar on Rosh Hashana, we elevate ourselves as a nation.

Story 3:
Inspiring future generations

Everybody needs to make sacrifices, whether parents for children or leaders for communities, for example. Some sacrifices are smaller, some are greater. We close with an example of the latter which provides some perspectives on one of our opening questions.

The ongoing sacrifices of the Israel Defence Forces (IDF) and their families, with God's help, are an embodiment of the Akeda in our generation. Their sacrifice is not only for Jews residing in Israel, as we have seen through events such as the incredible rescue at Entebbe in 1976.

IDF soldier Shmuel Akiva Wiess was only 20 years old when he was killed by terrorists in 2002 while serving in Jenin. His funeral took place on the following day, which was Yom HaShoah (Israeli Holocaust Memorial Day). His mother, Tzippora Wiess, said the following remarkable words at her son's funeral, less than 24 hours after his tragic death:

"Today is Yom HaShoah. Baruch Hashem (thank God), I gave birth to three healthy girls and six healthy boys - healthy children ready to serve our country. I always knew that there was a possibility of my sons not returning home. Six million Jews were killed in the Holocaust, amongst them were my grandparents, ten of their children, and four of their siblings. Jewish families and Jewish continuity is our response to the horrific Holocaust. My aunt lost her husband and son in the War of Independence of 1948, three years after the Holocaust ended. I can learn so much from her; she was proud of their sacrifice. I would like to publicly thank God for giving Shmuel the privilege of serving the State of Israel. For allowing him to live freely as a Jew in the country he loved. For enabling him to defend his people and country. My dear Shmuel, six million Jews who did die as soldiers salute you today. 'The Lord has given, and the Lord has taken; may the name of the Lord be blessed' Amen."

In the opening of this piece, we questioned why God no longer spoke to Avraham after the Akeda. On a personal note, for me, the words of Tzippora Wiess provide the strongest answer of all.

FUN FACTS FOR A REALLY RIDICULOUSLY RIVETING ROSH HASHANA

On Rosh Hashana we eat different types of food.

Why do we eat these foods?

We go 'behind the scenes' to find the reasons for eating them...

HONEY

Ever since the Jewish people were promised the Land of Israel as their homeland, they were promised a 'Land flowing with milk and honey'.

APPLE

When Isaac blessed Jacob he compared him to the sweet smell of a 'field' and our Rabbis from the Talmud identify this 'field' as an apple orchard.

In Mishlei (Proverbs), written by King Solomon, it describes 'apples of gold' and Shir Hashirim (Song of Songs) describes the apples' sweetness.

POMEGRANATE

Our good deeds over the past year and during the coming year should be as many as the seeds inside a pomegranate.

LADDER-SHAPED CHALLA

To represent life's 'ups and downs'.

CROWN-SHAPED CHALLA

To declare God as King of kings.

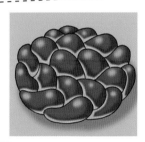

BIRD-SHAPED CHALLA

The prophet Isaiah described God's protection of the Jewish people as 'a hovering bird'.

ROUND CHALLA

We hope that the New Year will be 'rounded out in perfection'.

MORE FOOD FACTS >

CARROT

Carrots in Hebrew are 'Gezer', which sounds like G'zar, the Hebrew word for a 'Judgement' or a 'Decree'. We want all the bad judgements taken away and only good judgements remaining.

BEETROOT

Beetroot in Hebrew is 'Selek', similar to the word for "remove". We eat beetroot because we hope and pray that our enemies will be removed from us. In Aramaic, the language of the Talmud, 'silka' refers to a leafy green vegetable, similar to spinach.

BEANS

Beans, or even fenugreek is 'Rubia' in Hebrew, which is similar to the word 'Yirbu', "to increase". These foods give us hope for a fruitful year filled with increased goodness.

FISH HEAD

The head of a fish on the table is a sign of our hope that we are like a head and not a tail. We want to make progress in the coming year rather than hang around at the back!

LEEK

The Hebrew word for leek is related to the word 'karet', meaning to cut. We pray that those who wish to hurt us will be cut off.

DATE

Date honey is what the Torah is referring to when it describes the Land of Israel as "a land flowing with milk and honey".

TASHLICH

IS IT SOMETHING TO DO WITH A STREAM?

YES, THAT'S CORRECT!

On the first day of Rosh Hashana, or the second day if the first is Shabbat, we go to a nearby stream, river or even the sea (if it is nearby!) and 'empty' our pockets of all our sins!

It is a relatively new custom (13th century) with no direct biblical or Talmudic basis. The custom follows the prophet Micah's advice, 'You will throw all their sins into the depths of the sea.'

THE SHOFAR

There are so many customs that we do on Rosh Hashana, that it's easy to forget that on one of the most important days in the Jewish calendar, there is only ONE primary mitzvah (commandment), 'Hearing the Shofar'.

Shofar is a word which is derived from the name of an animal with a curved horn, reminding us of the ram's curved horn in the episode of the Binding of Isaac.
This episode is read on the second day of Rosh Hashana and is also mentioned in the Mussaf prayers.

We hear the sounds of the Shofar on each day of Rosh Hashana (unless the first day is a Shabbat). 100 notes are blown by the 'Ba'al Tokea' on each day of Rosh Hashana whilst the person who calls out the notes before they are blown is called the 'Ba'al Makreh'. These 100 notes are made up of four specific notes; Tekia, Shevarim, Terua and Tekia Gedolah.

SUPER
CUSTOMS FOR
ROSH HASHANA

DID YOU KNOW?
There are nine particularly symbolic foods eaten at Rosh Hashana. These are;

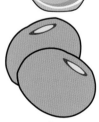

1. APPLES WITH
2. HONEY
3. LEEKS OR COURGETTE
4. BLACK-EYED PEAS
5. LAMB'S HEAD
6. BEETROOT
7. DATES
8. COW'S LUNG
9. POMEGRANATE

Although most of these foods are widely available in our shops, the lamb's head and cow's lungs can be hard to find!

Tongue is a Persian favourite and is often used instead of a lamb's head, while cow's lungs are often replaced with fish or popcorn!

This is because lung and fish meat are light and flaky and popcorn is also light. These things are eaten because we want the wrong things we have done during the year to be outweighed by all the good things we have done during the year.

THE SHOFAR

There is a Teimani (Yemenite) custom to only blow 51 notes of the Shofar on each day of Rosh Hashana.

Instead of a long Tekia (the long note of the shofar) being blown at the end of the service, Yemenite Jews blow a long Terua (a series of short notes).

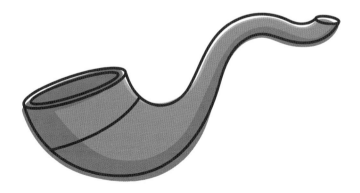

YOM KIPPUR FACTS

12/13+ Jewish people over the age of B'nei Mitzvah (12 for a girl and 13 for a boy) fast for 25 hours during Yom Kippur. We fast on this day because we want to be as pure as the angels who do not need to eat. We are also so engrossed in our prayers, that we do not have time to eat.

 The first of the 5 services of Yom Kippur is known as 'Kol Nidrei' ('All vows') and this Tefilla (Prayer) was composed in the 6th or 7th century. It was included in the first official siddur used in the 9th century.

12345 The 'Kol Nidrei' ('All Vows') prayer is the first of 5 prayer services we say on Yom Kippur. The morning service is called 'Shacharit', the additional service is called 'Musaf', the afternoon service is called 'Mincha' and the concluding service of Yom Kippur is known as 'Neila'.

 The Mincha (Afternoon) service on Yom Kippur has a very well-known Haftara (reading from the book of Prophets), which is all about Yona (Jonah). This Haftara is extremely appropriate for Yom Kippur, as it has as its running theme, the idea of Teshuva (Repentance).

 During the Neila (Concluding) Service the Ark is opened at the beginning and as we conclude the Neila service and Yom Kippur, the Ark is closed. When the Ark closes, it is as if the gates of heaven have closed, accepting all our prayers for a good year ahead.

At the end of the Neila Service and Yom Kippur, one long blast of the Shofar is blown (Tekia Gedola) and the congregation says, 'Next year in Jerusalem'. We say this phrase because of our hope that the ultimate redemption will occur in the month of Tishrei.

Whilst some Ashkenazi Jews wear a Kittel (White robe) on Yom Kippur, many in Sephardi communities do not. The Kittel demonstrates a desire to be free of all their wrong deeds and are willing to start the year anew.

A memorial service called 'Yizkor' is said in all Ashkenazi synagogues on Yom Kippur, but some Sephardi synagogues do not say 'Yizkor' on Yom Kippur.

OTHER FACTS ABOUT YOM KIPPUR

- The Yom Kippur War occurred in 1973, when Syria and Egypt attacked Israel on Yom Kippur hoping that the Israeli army would be distracted by the festival.

- People are also not supposed to wash, wear perfumes or wear leather shoes on this day, so that they can focus on the repentance of Yom Kippur.

- Children are not permitted to fast.

- Common greetings on Yom Kippur are "have an easy fast" or "well over the fast".

- The American Major League Baseball pitcher Sandy Koufax was Jewish. He decided not to pitch in game 1 of the World Series because it fell on Yom Kippur.

- The next major Jewish holiday after Yom Kippur is called Sukkot.

- Yom Kippur is the second of the High Holy Days after Rosh Hashana.

- Newly appointed Chelsea manager Avram Grant missed the club's preparations for its big match against Manchester United in 2007 because of the fast of Yom Kippur.

THE TRIBE SCRIBE

BUMPER YOM KIPPUR EPISODE: YONAH!

IN THE AFTERNOON OF YOM KIPPUR, DURING THE MINCHA SERVICE, WE READ THE BOOK OF YONAH.

YONAH WAS A PROPHET WHICH MEANS THAT GOD SPOKE TO HIM DIRECTLY. (NOW THAT'S PRETTY COOL!) GOD TOLD YONAH TO TRAVEL TO THE CITY OF NINEVEH WITH A MESSAGE FROM GOD. YONAH'S JOB WAS TO TELL THE PEOPLE OF NINEVEH TO STOP THEIR WICKED WAYS AND DO TESHUVA.

IT'S NOT JUST A FISHY TALE! JOIN US AS WE FIND OUT MORE ABOUT THE STORY OF YONAH, WHAT IT CAN MEAN TO US AND WHY WE READ IT ON YOM KIPPUR.

THAT SOUNDS STRAIGHTFORWARD! GET THE JOB, DO THE JOB, JOB DONE! OR NOT... INSTEAD OF TRAVELLING TO NINEVEH, YONAH RAN TO THE PORT AND BOARDED A SHIP TO TARSHISH – WHICH IS DEFINITELY NOT NINEVEH. DID HE GET THE WRONG BOAT? WHAT WAS THAT ABOUT?

YONAH DIDN'T WANT TO TALK TO THE PEOPLE OF NINEVEH AND HE DIDN'T THINK THEY WOULD LISTEN TO HIM ANYWAY. SO HE RAN AWAY. HE MUST HAVE KNOWN YOU CAN'T RUN FROM GOD!?!

Do ever feel overwhelmed by a job that seems too hard? What do YOU do about it?

THE SAILORS AND PASSENGER ARE WORRIED. THEY THROW TH LUGGAGE OVERBOARD TO MAK THE SHIP LIGHTER AND THEY PRAY TO THEIR GODS. YONAH GOES DOWN TO THE HOLD AND GOES TO SLEEP.

SO YONAH IS ON THE TARSHISH SHIP AND GOD IS NOT OK WITH THAT. GOD SENDS A HUGE STORM, WITH GALE FORCE WINDS AND ENORMOUS WAVES. THE SHIP LOOKS LIKE IT IS GOING TO CAPSIZE!

Have you ever gone to sleep to escape from something?

WAKE UP! HOW CAN YOU JUST SLEEP THROUGH THIS? GET UP AND PRAY. MAYBE YOUR GOD WILL SAVE US.

LOOK! THOSE OTHER SHIPS ARE IN CALM WATERS.

MAYBE IT'S A PUNISHMENT FOR SOMEONE ON OUR BOAT.

Of course the lottery landed on Yonah...

WHO ARE YOU AND WHAT HAVE YOU DONE TO BRING THIS TERRIBLE TEMPEST JUST OVER OUR SHIP?!

LET'S DRAW LOTS TO SEE WHOSE FAULT IT IS.